Dear Delegate,

Welcome to the Urbana 79 Missions Convention! We're glad you're here!

Urbana 79 is sponsored by the Inter-Varsity Christian Fellowships of the United States and Canada. Their primary purpose is to glorify Christ by helping students find God's place for them in world missions and thus to serve the church in strengthening its ministry. But Inter-Varsity is much more than Urbana.

Inter-Varsity Is Students

Inter-Varsity is students declaring God's glory on campuses, students living out their faith in Jesus Christ, students united by and rooted in Scripture, students reaching cross-culturally with the gospel.

Inter-Varsity is not a church, it is not a denomination, and it is not a mission board. *Inter-Varsity is part of the church as students and faculty from many denominations in hundreds of student-run campus fellowships commit themselves to follow Christ as Lord.*

What is this fellowship like? Each local "chapter" of IVCF strives to follow Jesus Christ in different ways. Many get together daily to praise God and to pray. In weekly Bible studies they dig into the Word for themselves. Students and faculty also encourage each other to share Christ with non-Christian friends. One faculty member shared Christ in his classes, and this encouraged students to share their faith. A dozen came to Christ as a result.

Inter-Varsity Is Training

But students and faculty are not alone. As a national movement IVCF provides many resources for campus Christians. Take, for example, one of the most important: Inter-Varsity staff members visit campuses to teach from the Scripture, to train in evangelism, to give an example of what it means to follow Christ daily. At one university, a staff member led a discipleship training program for a core of students; from this, students started an evangelistic Bible study and began personal evangelism; as a result, a new believer enrolled in the freshman discipleship course held soon after. The spiritual "cycle of life" continues.

Inter-Varsity students are also involved in training camps and conferences. The annual Fort Lauderdale Beach Evangelism Project at Easter, Bible and Life study weekends, and the summer-long Aspen Project are just a few of many.

Various branches of IVCF offer still other resources. The Student Missions Fellowship (SMF) works to present overseas missions at Christian schools. The

Nurses Christian Fellowship (NCF) shares the same goals as IVCF as it seeks to help nursing school students and graduates bring Christ into their nursing care. The TWENTYONEHUNDRED team produces multimedia shows for use on campus.

Committed discipleship is encouraged through literature. InterVarsity Press and HIS magazine both aim to help the mind grow under Christ's lordship.

Inter-Varsity Is a Worldwide Fellowship

Inter-Varsity in Canada and the United States are only two member movements of the worldwide International Fellowship of Evangelical Students (IFES). The movement in Brazil distributes Portuguese literature through bookstores, schools and newsstands in that country and in Portugal. In eight years, the Varsity Christian Fellowship at the U. of Singapore has grown from 40 students to over 900 through "contact groups" meeting for Bible study, prayer, fellowship and evangelism. Students in northern Cameroun are persevering despite Muslim domination and pagan hostility. West German high-school students raised approximately $1000 to assist new high-school work in Portugal and Mexico. Schloss Mittersill, a castle in the Austrian Alps, warmly welcomes the international family gathering for training conferences, Bible seminars, and evangelistic houseparties. These are only a few of the many activities of the over 50 national movements joined together in student outreach.

Inter-Varsity Is People

Inter-Varsity is more than Urbana—people on campus and off, salaried and volunteer, from many churches across North America; people behind the scenes, typing, keeping records, writing, planning, in national, regional and area offices; men and women entrusted with the corporate and legal responsibilities on the corporations and boards of IVCF-USA and IVCF-Canada; business people and homemakers serving on Local Committees to raise the funds needed to support the campus work—all these and more help make up Inter-Varsity.

We're glad you are here at Urbana. While you are here, we hope you will learn more about Inter-Varsity. Much more importantly, we hope you will learn what it means to believe and obey Jesus Christ on your campus, in your community, throughout the world.

Sincerely,

John W. Alexander
President, IVCF-U.S.A.

A. Donald MacLeod
General Director, IVCF-Canada

URBANA PRAISE

EDITED BY ROBERT FRYLING

INTER-VARSITY PRESS
DOWNERS GROVE
ILLINOIS 60515

FRED M.C. CHUNG
Urbana, IL

InterVarsity Press is the book-publishing
division of Inter-Varsity Christian Fellowship,
a student movement active on campus at
hundreds of universities, colleges and schools
of nursing. For information about local and
regional activities, write IVCF, 233 Langdon St.,
Madison, WI 53703.

Distributed in Canada through InterVarsity Press,
1875 Leslie St., Unit 10, Don Mills, Ontario
M3B 2M5, Canada.

ISBN 0-87784-585-9
Library of Congress Catalog Card
Number: 79-2717

Printed in the United States of America

Preface

Proclaim the Savior's name,
All we who know His grace;
Let every heart leap high with joy
To sound His praise!
Proclaim His risen life,
His glories blaze abroad,
That all His world may own Him Lord
And worship God!

For over three decades *Urbana* has meant student involvement in world missions. An involvement that requires vision, commitment, compassion and sacrifice; but also an involvement that lifts the soul to sing praises to God.

Thus the purpose of *Urbana Praise* is to provide a resource of spiritual songs that stimulates offerings of both praise and commitment to the Lord and Savior of the world. The simple structure of *Urbana Praise* reflects this dual purpose with the first section titled "Praise and Worship" and the second part, "Commitment and Service."

While care has been taken to select songs that are true to Scripture, we have also sought to represent various cultural expressions in music. This demonstrates the cultural diversity of the people of God and promotes greater sensitivity to different cultures for the sake of the gospel.

Urbana Praise is designed to be used in three ways. First, as the songbook for Urbana, Inter-Varsity's Student Missions Convention. Second, as a supplement to Inter-Varsity's major hymnbook, *Hymns II.* An index cross-references hymns found in both volumes, indicating where different tunes are used. Third, as a meaningful hymnbook in its own right; especially for Christians who want to "come into his presence with singing . . . and to serve the Lord with gladness."

Guitar chords have been included with most of the music. We have endeavored to keep the chords as simple as possible. To accomplish this it has been necessary, at times, to put the chords in a different key from the music, occasionally using different harmonizations as well. There is *no* notation of this in the music, but this should cause no difficulties unless other instruments are used. Parenthetical chords should be considered optional.

Every effort has been made to obtain proper copyrights. Any errors or omissions are unintentional and will be corrected in subsequent printings.

May *Urbana Praise* encourage and enable your heart to leap with joy and your life to proclaim to all people that Jesus Christ is Lord!

Robert Fryling
IVCF Staff, U.S.A.

PART I

WORSHIP PRAISE &

At the name of Jesus
Every knee shall bow,
Every tongue confess Him
King of Glory now;
'Tis the Father's pleasure
We should call Him Lord,
Who from the beginning
Was the mighty Word.

Carolina M Noel

O magnify the LORD with me, and let us exalt his name together/Ps 34:3

J E Seddon

Traditional spiritual
Let Us Break Bread

1. Let us praise God to-geth-er, Let us praise;
2. Let us seek God to-geth-er, Let us pray;
3. Let us serve God to-geth-er, Him o-bey;

Let us praise God to-geth-er All our days.
Let us seek His for-give-ness As we pray.
Let our lives show His good-ness Through each day.

He is faith-ful in all His ways, He is wor-thy of
He will cleanse us from all our sin, He will help us the
Christ the Lord is the world's true light, Let us serve Him with

all our praise, His name be ex-al-ted on high.
fight to win, His name be ex-al-ted on high.
all our might, His name be ex-al-ted on high.

To the . . . immortal, invisible, the only God, be honor and glory/1 Tim 1:17

Walter C Smith

Welsh melody
St Denio

1. Im - mor - tal, in - vi - si - ble, God on - ly wise,
2. Un - rest - ing, un - hast - ing, and si - lent as light,
3. To all, life thou giv - est, to both great and small,
4. Great Fa - ther of glo - ry, pure Fa - ther of light,

In light in - ac - ces - si - ble hid from our eyes,
Nor want - ing, nor wast - ing, thou rul - est in might;
In all life thou liv - est, the true life of all;
Thine an - gels a - dore thee, all veil - ing their sight;

Most bles - sed, most glo - rious, the An - cient of Days,
Thy jus - tice like moun - tains high soar - ing a - bove
We blos - som and flou - rish as leaves on the tree,
All praise we would ren - der: O help us to see

Al - might - y, vic - to - rious, thy great name we praise.
Thy clouds, which are foun - tains of good - ness and love.
And wi - ther and per - ish but naught chang - eth thee.
'Tis on - ly the splen - dor of light hid - eth thee. A - men.

3 The King of Glory

Praise & Worship

Lift up your heads, O gates! . . . that the King of glory may come in/Ps 24:7

W F Jabusch *Traditional Israeli folk song*

Refrain

The King of glo - ry comes, the na - tion re - joi - ces.

O - pen the gates be - fore Him, lift up your voi - ces.

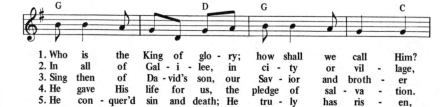

Verses

1. Who is the King of glo - ry; how shall we call Him?
2. In all of Gal - i - lee, in ci - ty or vil - lage,
3. Sing then of Da - vid's son, our Sav - ior and broth - er
4. He gave His life for us, the pledge of sal - va - tion.
5. He con - quer'd sin and death; He tru - ly has ris - en,

He is Em - man - u - el, the pro - mised of a - ges.
He goes a - mong His peo - ple cur - ing their ill - ness.
in all of Gal - i - lee was nev - er an - oth - er.
He took up - on Him - self the sins of the na - tion.
And He will share with us His heav - en - ly vi - sion.

Coda

The King of glo - ry comes, the na - tion re - joi - ces.

That . . . he might show the immeasurable riches of his grace
in kindness/Eph 2:7

Bryan Leech

Swedish melody
Elfåker

1. Kind and mer - ci - ful God, we have sinned in your sight,
2. Kind and mer - ci - ful God, we've ne - glect - ed your Word
3. Kind and mer - ci - ful God, we have bro - ken your laws
4. Kind and mer - ci - ful God, in Christ's death on the cross
5. Kind and mer - ci - ful God, bid us lift up our heads

We have all wan - dered far from your way;
And the truth that would guide us a - right;
And in con - duct have veered from the norm;
You pro - vid - ed a cleans - ing from sin;
And com - mand us to rise from our knees;

We have fol - lowed de - sire, We have failed to a - spire
We have lived in the shade Of the dark we have made,
We have dreamed of the good, But the good that we could
Speak the words that for - give That hence - forth we may live
May our hearts now be changed And no long - er es-tranged,

To the vir - tue we ought to dis - play.
When you willed us to walk in the light.
We have fre - quent - ly failed to per - form.
By the might of your Spi - rit with - in.
Through the pow'r of your par - don and peace. A - men.

The God of Abraham Praise

God reigns... on his holy throne... the God of Abraham/Ps 47:8-9

Yigdal of Daniel ben Judah
Thomas Olivers

Hebrew melody
arr Meyer Lyon
Leoni

1. The God of A-br'ham praise, Who reigns en-throned a-bove; An-cient of e-ver-last-ing days, And God of love. Je-ho-vah, great I AM, By earth and heav'n con-fessed; I bow and bless the sa-cred name, For-e-ver blest.

2. The God of A-br'ham praise, At whose su-preme com-mand From earth I rise, and seek the joys At His right hand. I all on earth for-sake, Its wis-dom, fame, and pow'r; And Him my on-ly por-tion make, My shield and tow'r.

3. He by Him-self hath sworn, I on His oath de-pend, I shall, on ea-gles' wings up-borne, To heav'n a-scend; I shall be-hold His face, I shall His pow'r a-dore, And sing the won-ders of His grace For-e-ver-more.

4. The whole tri-um-phant host Give thanks to God on high; "Hail, Fa-ther, Son and Ho-ly Ghost!" They e-ver cry. Hail, A-br'ham's God and mine! I join the heav'n-ly lays; All might and ma-jes-ty are Thine, And end-less praise. A-men.

The Lord is good to all/Ps 145:9

Source unknown   *African*

2. He cares for me, . . .   3. I'll do His will, . . .   4. He loves me so, . . .

I say to the LORD, "Thou art my Lord"/Ps 16:2

John B Foley   *John B Foley*

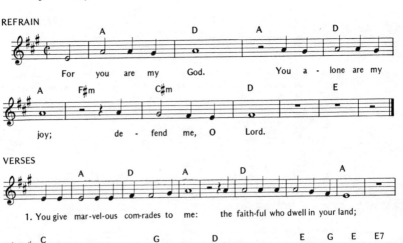

2. You are my por-tion and cup; it is you that I claim for my prize. Your
her-i-tage is my de-light: the lot you have giv-en to me. *to refrain*

3. Glad are my heart and my soul; se-cure-ly my bod-y shall rest. For
you will not leave me for dead; nor lead your be-lov-ed a-stray. *to refrain*

4. You show me the path for my life; in your pres-ence the full-ness of joy. To
be at your right hand for-ev-er for me would be hap-pi-ness al-ways. *to refrain*

8   Surely Goodness   Praise & Worship

I shall dwell in the house of the LORD for ever/Ps 23:6

Psalm 23:6   *John W Peterson*

   D
Surely goodness and mercy shall follow me
 A7   D
All the days, all the days of my life;

Surely goodness and mercy shall follow me
 A7   D
All the days, all the days of my life:
D7   G   D
and I shall dwell in the house of the LORD forever,
     Bm   E7   A
And I shall feast at the table spread for me:
A7   D
Surely goodness and mercy shall follow me
   A7   D
All the days, all the days of my life.

The high and lofty One . . . inhabits eternity, whose name is Holy/Is 57:15

Frederick W Faber

James Turle
Westminster

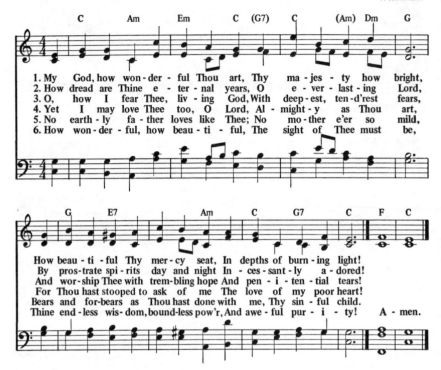

1. My God, how won-der-ful Thou art, Thy ma-jes-ty how bright,
2. How dread are Thine e-ter-nal years, O e-ver-last-ing Lord,
3. O, how I fear Thee, liv-ing God, With deep-est, ten-d'rest fears,
4. Yet I may love Thee too, O Lord, Al-might-y as Thou art,
5. No earth-ly fa-ther loves like Thee; No mo-ther e'er so mild,
6. How won-der-ful, how beau-ti-ful, The sight of Thee must be,

How beau-ti-ful Thy mer-cy seat, In depths of burn-ing light!
By pros-trate spi-rits day and night In-ces-sant-ly a-dored!
And wor-ship Thee with trem-bling hope And pen-i-ten-tial tears!
For Thou hast stooped to ask of me The love of my poor heart!
Bears and for-bears as Thou hast done with me, Thy sin-ful child.
Thine end-less wis-dom, bound-less pow'r, And awe-ful pur-i-ty! A-men.

---

10   **Make a Joyful Noise**   Praise & Worship
Psalm 100

Give thanks to him, bless his name!/Ps 100:4

Psalm 100

Source unknown

C(D)
1. Make a joyful noise unto the Lord,
   Am(Bm)
   All ye, all ye lands.
   F(G)
Serve the Lord, the Lord with gladness,
   G(A)
Come before His presence with singing.

2. Know ye that the Lord He is God:
   It is He that hath made us,
And not we ourselves.
   We are His people and the sheep
   of His pasture.

3. Enter into His gates with thanksgiving,
   And into His courts with praise;
Be thankful unto Him
   And bless, bless His name.

4. For the Lord, the Lord He is good;
   And His mercy is everlasting;
And His truth, His truth endureth,
   endureth to all generations.

5. Halleluia, glory halleluia!
   Halleluia, glory halleluia!
Halleluia, glory halleluia!
   Halleluia, glory halleluia!

Thou art my refuge, a strong tower against the enemy/Ps 61:3

Martin Luther   *Martin Luther*
tr Frederick H Hedge   *Ein Feste Burg*

1. A might-y For-tress is our God, A Bul-wark ne-ver fail - ing;
2. Did we in our own strength con-fide, Our striv-ing would be los - ing;
3. And though this world, with de-vils filled, Should threat-en to un-do us;
4. That word a-bove all earth-ly pow'rs, No thanks to them a-bi - deth;

Our Help-er He a-mid the flood Of mor-tal ills pre-vail - ing:
Were not the right Man on our side, The Man of God's own choos - ing:
We will not fear, for God hath willed His truth to tri-umph through us:
The Spi-rit and the gifts are ours Through Him who with us sid - eth:

For still our an-cient Foe Doth seek to work us woe; His craft and pow'r are great,
Dost ask who that way be? Christ Je-sus, it is He; Lord Sab-a-oth His Name,
The Prince of Dark-ness grim, We trem-ble not for him; His rage we can en-dure,
Let goods and kin-dred go, This mor-tal life al-so; The bo-dy they may kill;

And, armed with cru-el hate, On earth is not his e - qual.
From age to age the same, And He must win the bat - tle.
For lo! his doom is sure, One lit-tle word shall fell him.
God's truth a-bi-deth still, His King-dom is for-e - ver. A - men.

12 Father, I Adore You

Thou art our Father; we are the clay, and thou art our potter/Is 64:8

Terrye Coelho   *Terrye Coelho*

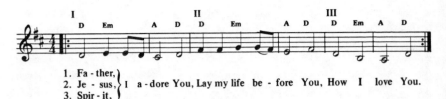

1. Fa - ther,
2. Je - sus, } I a - dore You, Lay my life be - fore You, How I love You.
3. Spir - it,

13 O Wondrous God

How Great Thou Art!

Great is the LORD and greatly to be praised/Ps 48:1

Carl Boberg   *Swedish folk tune*
tr Joseph T Bayly   *O Store Gud*

1. O wondrous God, when I Thy world consider,
Which Thou hast made by Thine almighty Word,
When I perceive the skill that leads my pathway,
The faithfulness that feeds me daily, Lord.

Refrain
Then soars my soul in joyful songs of praise,
    O wondrous God, how great Thou art!
Then soars my soul in joyful songs of praise,
    O wondrous God, how great Thou art!

2. When I behold the heavens stretching o'er me,
Where golden ships plow through the seas of blue,
Sun, moon and stars, all telling of Thy glory,
I see myself as less than dust or dew.

3. When in the storm I hear the voice of thunder
And lightning flashes swift across the sky,
When cold fresh winds blow in across the water
And rainbow glistens bright before my eye.

4. When from the storm I flee to find a shelter,
And see the lightning of Thy wrath set free,
Yet striking not at me the fallen sinner,
But flung against Thy Son upon a tree.

5. When storms are past, surpassing rainbow brightness,
Thou, Lord shall come to take me home with Thee;
Then I shall find that I am in Thy likeness,
Of grace a trophy for all worlds to see.

God, All Nature Sings Thy Glory

The heavens are telling the glory of God/Ps 19:1

David Clowney

Ludwig van Beethoven
Ode to Joy

1. God, all nature sings Thy glory, And Thy works proclaim Thy might;
2. Clearer still we see Thy hand in Man whom Thou hast made for Thee;
3. But our sins have spoiled Thine image; Nature, conscience only serve
4. God of glory, power, mercy, All creation praises Thee;

Ordered vastness in the heavens, Ordered course of day and night;
Ruler of creation's glory, Image of Thy Majesty.
As unceasing, grim reminders Of the wrath which we deserve.
We, Thy creatures, would adore Thee Now and through eternity.

Beauty in the changing seasons, Beauty in the storming sea;
Music, art, the fruitful garden, All the labor of his days,
Yet Thy grace and saving mercy In Thy Word of truth revealed
Saved to magnify Thy goodness, Grant us strength to do Thy will;

All the changing moods of nature Praise the changeless Trinity.
Are the calling of his Maker To the harvest feast of praise.
Claim the praise of all who know Thee, In the blood of Jesus sealed.
With our acts as with our voices Thy commandments to fulfill. Amen.

Esperanza mia, y castillo mio; mi Dios, en quien confiaré/Sal 91:2

Luz E Cuna

Rafael Cuna
arr Norman Johnson

1. El que ha-bi - ta al a - bri - go de Dios___ Mo-ra-
2. El que ha-bi - ta al a - bri - go de Dios___ Cier-ta-
3. El que ha-bi - ta al a - bri - go de Dios___ Pa-ra

rá ba-jo som-bras de a - mor;___ So-bre él no ven-drá nin-gún
men-te muy fe-liz se - rá;___ An-ge-les guar-da-rán su sa-
siem-pre se-gu-ro es-ta - rá;___ Ca-e-rán mil y diez mil por

mal___ Y en sus a - las fe - liz vi-vi-rá.___
lud___ Y sus pies nun-ca res-ba-la-rán.___
do - quier, Mas a él no ven-drá mor-tan-dad.___

CORO
Oh, yo quie-ro ha-bi-tar al a - bri-go de Dios, Só-lo a-llí en-con-tra-

ré paz y pro-fun-do a-mor. Mi de-li - cia con El co-mu-

nión dis-fru-tar Y yo siem-pre su nom-bre a-la - bar.

16 He Who Dwells

Praise & Worship

Under his wings you will find refuge/Ps 91:4

English words to El Que Habita *(hymn 15)*

1. He who dwells in the shelter of God
Shall find shade and inhabit in love.
He shall not be accosted by evil,
But shall happily live in His wings.

Chorus:
O, I want so to live in the shelter of God,
Only there might I find true peace
   and depths of love.
My delight is with Him
In communion to joy,
And to ever sing praise to His name.

2. He who dwells in the shelter of God
Shall most surely in happiness be,
And the angels shall watch for his health,
And his feet shall not slip on the ground.

3. He who dwells in the shelter of God
In security always shall live.
Thousands and tens of thousands shall fall,
But for him death shall never arrive.

17 Awake, O Israel

Praise & Worship

The Deliverer will come from Zion/Rom 11:26

Source unknown

Traditional

1. Awake, O Israel, put off thy slumber
For the truth shall set you free.
From out of Zion comes thy deliverer
In the year of jubilee.

2. Thou art my chosen, for I have sought
   thee;
Thou art graven on my hand.
And I will gather all those who scatter
And return them to their land.

3. Out of the furnace of much affliction
I have chosen thee, behold.
And for iron I'll give thee silver
And for brass I'll give thee gold.

4. Oh Alleluia! Oh Alleluia!
Alleluia—Praise the Lord!
Oh Alleluia! Oh Alleluia!
Alleluia—Praise the Lord!

O God, Our Help in Ages Past

Lord, thou hast been our dwelling place in all generations/Ps 90:1

Isaac Watts

William Croft
St Anne

1. O God, our help in a - ges past, Our hope for years to come,
2. Un - der the sha - dow of Thy throne Still may we dwell se - cure;
3. Be - fore the hills in or - der stood, Or earth re - ceived her frame,
4. A thou - sand a - ges in Thy sight Are like an eve - ning gone;
5. O God, our help in a - ges past, Our hope for years to come,

Our shel - ter from the storm - y blast, And our e - ter - nal home!
Suf - fi - cient is Thine arm a - lone, And our de - fense is sure.
From e - ver - last - ing Thou art God, To end - less years the same.
Short as the watch that ends the night, Be - fore the ris - ing sun.
Be Thou our guide while life shall last, And our e - ter - nal home! A - men.

19 Thy Lovingkindness

Thy steadfast love is better than life/Ps 63:3

Psalm 63:3-4

Source unknown

Women:

1. Thy lov - ing - kind - ness is
2. I lift my hands up

Men:

1. Thy lov - ing - kind - ness is bet - ter than life.
2. I lift my hands up in thy name.

3. I lift my voice up in Thy name.
I lift my voice up in Thy name.
My lips shall praise Thee.
Thus will I bless Thee.
I will lift up my voice in Thy name.

4. I lift my eyes up in Thy name.
I lift my eyes up in Thy name.
My lips shall praise Thee.

Thus will I bless Thee.
I will lift up my eyes in Thy name.

5. I lift my heart up in Thy name.
I lift my heart up in Thy name.
My lips shall praise Thee.
Thus will I bless Thee.
I will lift up my heart in Thy name.

I saw the Lord sitting upon a throne, high and lifted up/Is. 6:1

Isaiah 6:1, 3   *Source unknown*

I see the Lord. I see the Lord; He is high and lift-ed up, and His train fills the tem-ple. He is high and lift-ed up, and His train fills the tem-ple. The an-gels cry "Ho-ly". The an-gels cry "Ho-ly". The an-gels cry "Ho-ly is the Lord."

arrangement: Reprinted from HIGH PRAISE, *compiled by Jonathan Lyle,* © *1977 by Harold Shaw Publishers, Box 567, Wheaton, Illinois 60187. Used by permission.*

21 **Glorious Is Your Name**

Blessed be his glorious name for ever/Ps 72:19

Ruth Elliot

Franz Joseph Haydn
Austrian hymn

1. Glo-rious is your name, Most Ho-ly, God and Fa-ther of us all;
2. For our world of need and an-guish We would lift to you our prayer.
3. In the midst of time we jour-ney; From your hand comes each new day:

We, your ser-vants, bow be-fore you, Strive to an-swer ev-ery call.
Faith-ful stew-ards of your boun-ty, May we with our broth-ers share.
We would use it in your serv-ice, Hum-bly, wise-ly, while we may.

You with life's great good have blest us, Cared for us from ear-liest years;
In the name of Christ our Sav-ior, Who re-deems and sets us free,
So to you, Lord and Cre-a-tor, Praise and hon-or we ac-cord!

Un-to you our thanks we ren-der; Your deep love o'er-comes all fears.
Gifts we bring of heart and trea-sure, That our lives may wor-thier be.
Yours the earth and yours the heav-ens, Through all time the e-ter-nal Word. A-men.

I love thee, O LORD, my strength/Ps 18:1

Richard Bewes

Richard Bewes
arr Christian Strover

waves were sweep-ing me a - way; In dis - tress I called on my

God for help, With - in His house He heard my cry.

D.C. al fine

2. The earth was rocking below, the mountains trembled in fear,
They shook and reeled beneath the wrath of God!
With smoke His breathing came forth, His mouth with scorching gave heat;
He rent the skies! Descended and came down!
    And the righteous God set me over them,
    Subdued the enemies I feared;
    He exalted me up above my foes,
    Delivered me from violent men!

3. I'll bring You praises, O Lord, among the nations of earth,
And to Your Name I'll sing a psalm of love!
Your love is steadfast and sure, and victory follows Your own—
You are our King—both now and evermore!

23 I Will Sing unto the Lord

The Horse and Rider

Praise & Worship

I will sing to the LORD, for he has triumphed gloriously/Ex 15:1

Exodus 15:1-2

Traditional round

1.C.   Am   F   Dm7
I will sing unto the Lord, for He has triumphed gloriously:
    G7   C
The horse and rider thrown into the sea. *(Repeat)*
2.   C   Am   F   Dm7
The Lord, my God, my strength, my song,
    G7   C
Is now become my victory. *(Repeat)*
3.   C   Am   F   Dm7
The Lord is God and I will praise Him,
    G7   C(G)   G7(C)
My father's God and I will exalt Him! *(Repeat)*

(Repeat using parenthetical chords last time)

The Twenty-Third Psalm

I shall dwell in the house of the LORD for ever/Ps 23:6

Psalm 23   *Ancient Chinese tune*
English arr W Hines Sims

1. Ye - he - wa shi wo mu - zhe, wo bi bu zhi que - fa,
2. Wo sui - ran xing - guo si - yin - de yu - gu, ye bu pa zao - hai, yin - wei Ni
3. Wo yi sheng yi shi, wo yi sheng yi shi, bi you en - hui, bi you en - hui

1. The Lord is my shep - herd; I shall not want, I shall not want.
2. Yea, tho' I walk thro' the val - ley, Yea, tho' I walk thro' the val - ley,
3. Thou pre - par - est a ta - ble be - fore me In the pres - ence of my en - e - mies:

Ta shi wo tang - wo zai qing caodi shang, ling wo zai ke - an - xie di shui bian,
Yu wo tong zai, Ni - de zhang, Ni - de gan dou an - hui wo.
Ci - ai sui - zhe wo, Wo yi sheng yi - shi, bi you en - hui ci - ai sui - zhe wo.

He mak - eth me, He mak - eth me to lie down in green pas - tures:
Yea, tho' I walk, thro' the val - ley of the shad - ow of death,
Thou a - noint - est my head, my head with oil; my cup run - neth o - ver.

Ta shi wo - di ling - hun su - xing, wei zi - ji di ming yin - dao wo zou yi lu,
Zai wo di - ren mian - qian, Ni wei wo bai - she yen - xi, Ni yong you gao - le wo - de tou.
Bi you en - hui ci - ai sui - zhe wo, wo qie yao zhu zai ye - he - wa - di dian zhong,

He lead - eth me be - side the still wa - ters. He re - stor - eth my soul: He re - stor - eth my soul:
I will fear no e - vil for Thou art with me; Thy rod and Thy staff they com - fort me.
Sure - ly good - ness and mer - cy shall fol - low me all the days, all the days of my life:

wei zi - ji di ming   yin-dao wo   zou yi lu,   yin-dao wo zou yi   lu.
shi wo-de fu   bei   man   -   yi,   wo-de fu bei man   -   yi.
wo   qie yao zhu zai ye- he-wa-di dian zhong, zhi   dao   yong   yuan.
He   lead-eth me   in the paths of right-eous-ness for   His   name's   sake.
Thy rod and Thy staff they   com - fort me, they com   -   fort   me.
and   I will dwell in the house of the Lord   for - ev   -   er.

25   **Praise to the Lord, the Almighty**   Praise & Worship

The LORD has established his throne in the heavens, and his kingdom rules over all/Ps 103:19

Joachim Neander   *"Stralsund Gesangbuch" (1665)*
tr Catherine Winkworth   *Lobe den Herren*

G   D   G   Bm   G   C   EmD-7 G
1. Praise to the Lord, the Almighty, the King of creation!
G   D   G   Bm   G   C   Em D-7 G
O my soul, praise Him, for He is thy health and salvation!
G   C
All ye who hear,
G   D   G   D
Now to His temple draw near;
G   F#m Em G A/C D7 G
Praise Him in glad adoration!

2. Praise to the Lord! who o'er all things so wondrously reigneth,
Shelters thee under His wings, yea, so gently sustaineth;
Hast thou not seen
How thy entreaties have been
Granted in what He ordaineth?

3. Praise to the Lord! who doth prosper thy work and defend thee;
Surely His goodness and mercy here daily attend thee.
Ponder anew
What the Almighty can do,
If with His love He befriend thee.

4. Praise to the Lord! O let all that is in me adore Him!
All that hath life and breath, come now with praises before Him!
Let the Amen
Sound from His people again;
Gladly for aye we adore Him. Amen.

Because the Lord Is My Shepherd

The New Twenty-Third

The LORD is my shepherd, I shall not want/Ps 23:1

Ralph Carmichael   Ralph Carmichael

Be-cause the Lord is my shep-herd I have ev-'ry-thing that I need.____ He lets me rest in mead-ows green and____ leads__ me be-side the qui-et stream. He keeps on giv-ing life to me and__ helps__ me to do what hon-ors Him the most. E-ven when walk-ing thru the dark val-ley__ of death, val-ley of death,____ I will nev-er be a-fraid, for He__ is close be-side__ me. Guard-ing, guid-ing all the way, He spreads a feast be-fore__me__ In the pres-ence of my en-e-mies He__ wel-comes me As His spec-ial guest with bless-ing o-ver flow-ing, His good-ness and un-fail-ing kind-ness shall__be

with me all of my life.___ And af-ter-wards I shall live with Him for ev - er, for ev - er_____ In___ His home,_____ for ev - er in___ His home. For ev - er in___ His home.

27   I Will Sing of the Mercies   Praise & Worship

I will sing of thy steadfast love, O LORD, for ever/Ps 89:1

Psalm 89:1

Source unknown

   C
I will sing of the mercies of the Lord forever,
  G   C
I will sing, I will sing,

I will sing of the mercies of the Lord forever,
  G   C
I will sing of the mercies of the Lord.

        F   C
With my mouth will I make known
  G7   C
Thy faithfulness, Thy faithfulness,
        F   C
With my mouth will I make known
  G   D7 G7
Thy faithfulness to all generations.

   C
I will sing of the mercies of the Lord forever,
  G   C
I will sing of the mercies of the Lord.

28   Therefore the Redeemed of the Lord   Praise & Worship

The ransomed of the LORD shall return, and come to Zion with singing/Is 51:11

Isaiah 51:11   *Ruth Lake*

    A   Amaj7   A7
1. Therefore the redeemed of the Lord shall return,
                 D
And come with singing unto Zion;
        A   F#m   Bm   E7   A
And everlasting joy shall be upon their head.

    A   Amaj7   A7
2. Therefore the redeemed of the Lord shall return,
                 D
And come with singing unto Zion;
        A   F#m   D6   E   A
And everlasting joy shall be upon their head.

   A7   D   A
3. They shall obtain gladness and joy;
   B7   E7
and sorrow and mourning shall flee away.
(Repeat vs. 1)

29   Children of the Heavenly Father   Praise & Worship

As a father pities his children, so the LORD pities/Ps 103:13

Lina Sandell   *Swedish melody*
tr Ernst Olsen   *arr Marc Hedlin*
                                   Tryggare Kan Ingen Vara

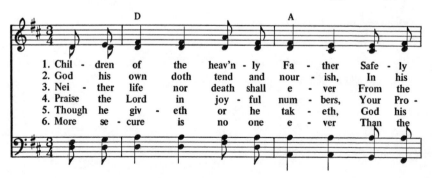

1. Chil - dren   of   the   heav'n - ly   Fa - ther   Safe - ly   In   his
2. God   his   own   doth   tend   and   nour - ish,   In   his
3. Nei - ther   life   nor   death   shall   e - ver   From   the
4. Praise   the   Lord   in   joy - ful   num - bers,   Your   Pro -
5. Though   he   giv - eth   or   he   tak - eth,   God   his
6. More   se - cure   is   no   one   e - ver   Than   the

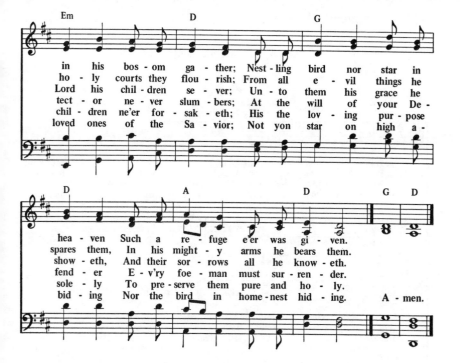

in his bos - om ga - ther; Nest - ling bird nor star in
ho - ly courts they flou - rish; From all e - vil things he
Lord his chil - dren se - ver; Un - to them his grace he
tect - or ne - ver slum - bers; At the will of your De -
chil - dren ne'er for - sak - eth; His the lov - ing pur - pose
loved ones of the Sa - vior; Not yon star on high a -

hea - ven Such a re - fuge e'er was gi - ven.
spares them, In his might - y arms he bears them.
show - eth, And their sor - rows all he know - eth.
fend - er E - v'ry foe - man must sur - ren - der.
sole - ly To pre - serve them pure and ho - ly.
bid - ing Nor the bird in home - nest hid - ing. A - men.

from the Lutheran Service Book and Hymnal *by permission of the Commission on the Liturgy and Hymnal;*
arrangement: © *1976 Marc Hedlin, assigned to Inter-Varsity Christian Fellowship.*

30   This Is the Day

Praise & Worship

This is the day which the LORD has made/Ps 118:24

Psalm 118:24

Maori folk tune

   D   A7 D   A7 D
1. This is the day, this is the day
        A
That the Lord hath made, that the Lord hath made;

We will rejoice, we will rejoice
      D   D7
And be glad in it, and be glad in it.
  G   D A7 D7
  This is the day that the Lord hath made;
  G   D A D
  We will rejoice and be glad in it.
    A7 D   A7
This is the day, this is the day
D G   D A7   D
That the Lord hath made.

2. This is the day when he rose again.

3. This is the day when the Spirit came.

Praise, My Soul

Bless the LORD, O my soul, and forget not all his benefits/Ps 103:2

Henry F Lyte

John Goss
Lauda Anima

1. Praise, my soul, the King of hea - ven, To His feet your
2. Praise Him for His grace and fa - vor To our fa - thers
3. Fa - ther - like, He tends and spares us, Well our fee - ble
4. An - gels help us to a - dore Him, You be - hold Him

tri - bute bring; Ran - somed, healed, re - stored, for - gi - ven,
in dis - tress; Praise Him, still the same for e - ver,
frame He knows; In His hands He gen - tly bears us,
face to face; Sun and moon, bow down be - fore Him;

Who, like me, His praise should sing? Al - le - lu - ia!
Slow to chide, and swift to bless; Al - le - lu - ia!
Res - cues us from all our foes; Al - le - lu - ia!
Dwel - lers all in time and space, Al - le - lu - ia!

Al - le - lu - ia! Praise the e - ver - last - ing King!
Al - le - lu - ia! Glo - rious in His faith - ful - ness!
Al - le - lu - ia! Wide - ly as His mer - cy flows!
Al - le - lu - ia! Praise with us the God of grace! A - men

The world was created by the word of God/Heb 11:3

R T Brooks

John Goss
Lauda Anima (hymn 31)

1. Thanks to God whose Word was spoken
   In the deed that made the earth.
His the voice that called a nation;
   His the fires that tried her worth.
God has spoken; God has spoken;
   Praise Him for His open Word.

2. Thanks to God whose Word incarnate
   Glorified the flesh of man.
Deeds and words and death and rising
   Tell the grace in heaven's plan.
God has spoken; God has spoken;
   Praise Him for His open Word.

3. Thanks to God whose Word is answered
   By the Spirit's voice within.
Here we drink of joy unmeasured,
   Life redeemed from death and sin.
God is speaking; God is speaking;
   Praise Him for His open Word. Amen.

words used by permission of R. T. Brooks, 1918-

33   **Alleluia!**   Praise & Worship

Once more they cried, "Hallelujah!"/Rev 19:3

Source unknown   *Source unknown*

1. Al - le - lu - ia, al - le - lu - ia, al - le - lu - ia, al - le - lu - ia,

al - le - lu - ia, al - le - lu - ia, al - le - lu - ia, al - le - lu - ia!

2. He's my Savior, . . .   3. I will praise Him, . . .   4. He is worthy, . . .

34   The Law of the Lord Is Perfect

The law of the LORD is perfect, reviving the soul/Ps 19:7

Psalm 19:7-11   *Source unknown*

     D   Em
1. The law of the Lord is perfect,
  A7   D
  converting the soul:
       Em   A7
The testimony of the Lord is sure,
           D
  making wise the simple.

Refrain
        G   A7
More to be desired are they than gold,
         F#m
  yea, than much fine gold:
Bm   Em7
Sweeter also than honey
    A7   D
  and the honey comb.
(to Coda last time only)

2. The statutes of the Lord are right,
   rejoicing the heart:
The commandment of the Lord is pure,
   enlightening the eyes,

3. The fear of the Lord is clean,
   enduring forever:
The judgments of the Lord are true
   and righteous altogether.

Coda (last time only)
                      G   A7
Moreover by them is thy servant warned,
            F#m
  is thy servant warned.
Bm   Em7
  and in keeping of them
    A7   D
  is great reward.

---

35   I Will Put My Laws

Praise & Worship

The New Covenant

I will put my laws into their minds/Heb 8:10

Robert C Loveless   *Hawaiian melody*
                                         Robert C Loveless

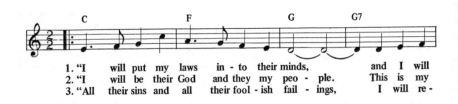

1. "I will put my laws in-to their minds, and I will
2. "I will be their God and they my peo - ple. This is my
3. "All their sins and all their fool-ish fail - ings, I will re -

write them on their hearts, I will write them on their
cov - e - nant with you, my new cov - e - nant with
mem - ber them no more, will re - mem - ber them no

hearts," says the Lord.
more," says the Lord.

you," says the Lord,

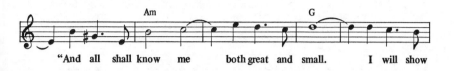

"And all shall know me both great and small. I will show

mer - cy to an - y - one who on my name shall call."

36   Kum Ba Yah

Praise & Worship

I will not leave you desolate; I will come to you/Jn 14:18

African (Angola)

African (Angola)

    C   F   C
1. Kum ba yah, my Lord, Kum ba yah!
                     F   G
Kum ba yah, my Lord, Kum ba yah!
  C   F   C
Kum ba yah, my Lord, Kum ba yah!
F C   G   C
O Lord, Kum ba yah.

2. Someone's crying, Lord, Kum ba yah!
Someone's crying, Lord, Kum ba yah!
Someone's crying, Lord, Kum ba yah!
O Lord, Kum ba yah.

3. Someone's singing, Lord, Kum ba yah!
Someone's singing, Lord, Kum ba yah!
Someone's singing, Lord, Kum ba yah!
O Lord, Kum ba yah.

4. Someone's praying, Lord, Kum ba yah!
Someone's praying, Lord, Kum ba yah!
Someone's praying, Lord, Kum ba yah!
O Lord, Kum ba yah.

Heaven and earth will pass away, but my words will not pass away/Lk 21:33

Rippon's "Selection of Hymns" (1787)   *Traditional American melody*
Foundation

1. How firm a foun - da - tion, ye saints of the Lord,
2. "Fear not, I am with thee, O be not dis - mayed,
3. "When through the deep wa - ters I call thee to go,
4. "When through fier - y tri - als thy path - way shall lie,
5. "The soul that on Je - sus hath leaned for re - pose,

Is laid for your faith in His ex - cel - lent word!
For I am thy God, and will still give thee aid;
The riv - ers of sor - row shall not o - ver - flow;
My grace, all - suf - fi - cient, shall be thy sup - ply;
I will not, I will not de - sert to his foes;

What more can He say than to you He hath said,
I'll strength - en thee, help thee, and cause thee to stand,
For I will be with thee, thy trou - bles to bless,
The flame shall not hurt thee; I on - ly de - sign
That soul, though all hell should en - dea - vor to shake,

To you who for re - fuge to Je - sus have fled.
Up - held by My right - eous, om - ni - po - tent hand.
And sanc - ti - fy to thee thy deep - est dis - tress.
Thy dross to con - sume, and thy gold to re - fine.
I'll ne - ver, no ne - ver, no ne - ver for - sake!" A - men.

Christ Is the Rock

Praise & Worship

He only is my rock and my salvation/Ps 62:2

adpt Ruth Lewis

Puerto Rican melody

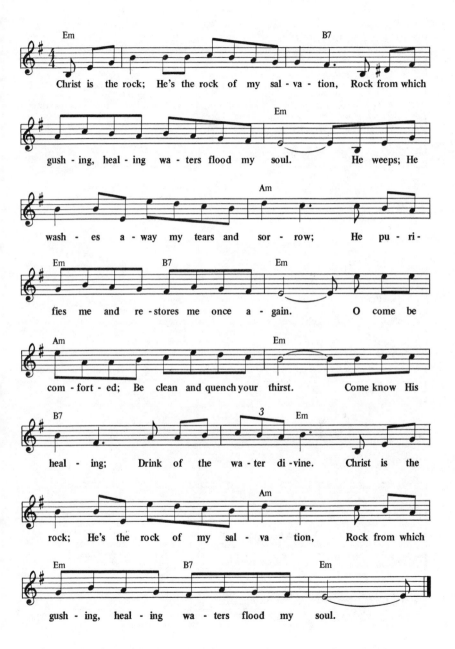

God has . . . bestowed on him the name which is above every name/Phil 2:9

Charles Wesley   *Thomas Phillips*
                                                                         Lydia

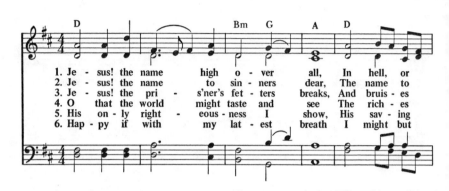

1. Je - sus! the name   high   o - ver   all,   In   hell, or
2. Je - sus! the name   to   sin - ners   dear,   The   name to
3. Je - sus! the pri - s'ner's fet - ters breaks, And   bruis - es
4. O   that the world   might taste and   see   The   rich - es
5. His   on - ly right - eous - ness   I   show,   His   sav - ing
6. Hap - py if   with   my   lat - est   breath   I   might but

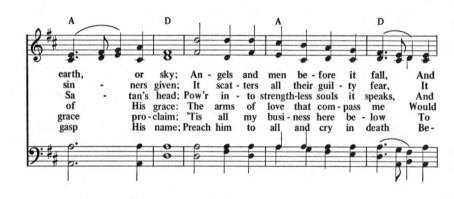

earth,   or   sky;   An - gels and men be - fore   it   fall,   And
sin - ners given;   It   scat - ters all   their guil - ty fear,   It
Sa - tan's head; Pow'r in - to strength-less souls   it   speaks,   And
of   His   grace: The   arms   of   love that com - pass me   Would
grace   pro - claim; 'Tis   all   my busi - ness here be - low   To
gasp   His   name; Preach him   to   all   and cry   in death   Be -

de - vils fear and   fly,   And de - vils   fear   and   fly.
turns their hell to heav'n,   It turns their   hell   to   heav'n.
life   in - to   the dead,   And life   in - to   the   dead.
all man-kind em - brace, Would all   man - kind   em - brace.
cry: Be - hold the Lamb!   To   cry: Be - hold   the   Lamb!
hold, be - hold the Lamb!   Be - hold, be - hold   the   Lamb!

Christ, our paschal lamb, has been sacrificed/1 Cor 5:7

Source unknown *Traditional round*

At the name of Jesus every knee should bow/Phil 2:10

Carolina M. Noel   *Ralph Vaughan Williams*
                                                         King's Weston

1. At the name of Je - sus Ev - ery knee shall bow,
2. At His voice cre - a - tion Sprang at once to sight,
3. Hum - bled for a sea - son, To re - ceive a name
4. In your hearts en - throne Him; There let Him sub - due
5. Broth - ers, this Lord Je - sus Shall re - turn a - gain,

Ev - ery tongue con - fess Him King of Glo - ry now;
All the an - gel fac - es, All the hosts of light,
From the lips of sin - ners, Un - to whom He came,
All that is not ho - ly, All that is not true:
With His Fa - ther's glo - ry O'er the earth to reign;

'Tis the Fa - ther's pleas - ure We should call Him Lord,
Thrones and dom - i - na - tions, Stars up - on their way,
Faith - ful - ly He bore it Spot - less to the last,
Crown Him as your Cap - tain In temp - ta - tion's hour;
For all wreaths of em - pire Meet up - on His brow,

Who from the be - gin - ning Was the might - y Word.
All the heav'n - ly or - ders In their great ar - ray.
Brought it back vic - to - rious, When from death He passed.
Let His will en - fold you In its light and power.
And our hearts con - fess Him King of Glo - ry now. A - men.

music: from Enlarged Songs of Praise *by permission of Oxford University Press.*

42 I Am the Resurrection

Jesus said to her, "I am the resurrection and the life"/Jn 11:25

Ray Repp   *Ray Repp*

Chorus

A   Em   A   Em
I am the resurrection and the life;
C   D   C   A
He who believes in Me will never die.
A   Em   A   Em
I am the resurrection and the life;
C   D   C   A
He who believes in Me will live a new life.

        G   D   A
1. I have come to bring the truth;

G   D   A
I have come to bring you life;
G   D   C   A
If you believe, then you shall live.

2. In My word all men shall come to know
It is love which makes the spirit grow.
If you believe, then you shall live.

3. Keep in mind the things that I have said;
Remember Me in the breaking of the bread.
If you believe, then you shall live.

43 O for a Thousand Tongues

Then my tongue shall tell of . . . thy praise all the day long/Ps 35:28

Charles Wesley   *Carl Gläser*
                                      arr Lowell Mason
                                          Azmon

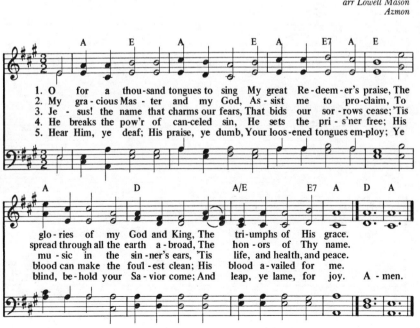

1. O for a thou-sand tongues to sing My great Re-deem-er's praise, The
2. My gra-cious Mas-ter and my God, As-sist me to pro-claim, To
3. Je-sus! the name that charms our fears, That bids our sor-rows cease; 'Tis
4. He breaks the pow'r of can-celed sin, He sets the pri-s'ner free; His
5. Hear Him, ye deaf; His praise, ye dumb, Your loos-ened tongues em-ploy; Ye

glo-ries of my God and King, The tri-umphs of His grace.
spread through all the earth a-broad, The hon-ors of Thy name.
mu-sic in the sin-ner's ears, 'Tis life, and health, and peace.
blood can make the foul-est clean; His blood a-vailed for me.
blind, be-hold your Sa-vior come; And leap, ye lame, for joy. A-men.

And Can It Be

While we were yet sinners Christ died for us/Rom 5:8

Charles Wesley

Thomas Campbell
Sagina

1. And can it be that I should gain An in-t'rest in the Sa-vior's blood? Died He for me, who caused His pain? For me, who Him to death pur-sued? A-maz-ing love! how can it be That Thou, my God, shouldst die for me? A-maz-ing love! how

2. 'Tis mys-t'ry all! Th'Im-mor-tal dies: Who can ex-plore His strange de-sign? In vain the first-born ser-aph tries To sound the depths of love di-vine. 'Tis mer-cy all! let earth a-dore, Let an-gel minds in-quire no more. 'Tis mer-cy all! let

3. He left His Fa-ther's throne a-bove, So free, so in-fi-nite His grace, Emp-tied Him-self of all but love, And bled for A-dam's help-less race. 'Tis mer-cy all, im-mense and free; For, O my God, it found out me! 'Tis mer-cy all, im-

4. Long my im-pri-son'd spi-rit lay Fast bound in sin and na-ture's night; Thine eye dif-fused a quick-'ning ray, I woke, the dun-geon flamed with light; My chains fell off, my heart was free, I rose, went forth, and fol-lowed Thee. My chains fell off, my

5. No con-dem-na-tion now I dread; Je-sus, and all in Him, is mine! A-live in Him, my liv-ing Head, And clothed in right-eous-ness di-vine, Bold I ap-proach th'e-ter-nal throne, And claim the crown, through Christ, my own. Bold I ap-proach th'e-
A-maz-ing love!

can it be That Thou, my God, shouldst die for me?
earth a - dore, Let an - gel minds in - quire no more.
mense and free; For, O my God, it found out me!
heart was free, I rose, went forth, and fol - lowed Thee.
ter - nal throne, And claim the crown, through Christ, my own. A - men.

How can it be That Thou my God

45 Jesus Shall Reign

Praise & Worship

May he have dominion from sea to sea/Ps 72:8

Isaac Watts

John Hatton

1. Je - sus shall reign wher - e'er the sun Does his suc -
2. Bles - sings a - bound wher - e'er He reigns The pri - s'ner
3. To Him shall end - less prayer be made, And end - less
4. Peo - ple and realms of e - v'ry tongue Dwell on His

ces - sive jour - neys run; His king - dom spread from shore to
leaps to lose his chains; The wea - ry find e - ter - nal
prais - es crown His head; His name like sweet per - fume shall
love with sweet - est song, And in - fant voic - es shall pro -

shore, Till moons shall wax and wane no more.
rest, And all the sons of want are blest.
rise With e - v'ry morn - ing sac - ri - fice.
claim Their ear - ly bles - sings on His name. A - men.

Come Go with Me to That Land

Praise & Worship

We are setting out for the place of which the LORD said,
"I will give it to you"/Num 10:29

Source unknown   *Traditional*

He has a name inscribed, King of kings and Lord of lords/Rev 19:16

Edward Perronet   *James Ellor*
stanza 4 John Rippon   *Diadem*

1. All hail the pow'r of Je - sus' name! Let an - gels pros - trate
2. Ye cho - sen seed of Is - rael's race; Ye ran - somed from the
3. Sin - ners, whose love can ne'er for - get The worm-wood and the
4. Let e - v'ry kin - dred, e - v'ry tribe, On this ter - res - trial
5. O that with yon - der sa - cred throng We at His feet may

fall, Let an - gels pros - trate fall; Bring forth the ro - yal
fall, Ye ran - somed from the fall; Hail Him who saves you
gall, The worm - wood and the gall, Go, spread your tro - phies
ball, On this ter - res - trial ball, To Him all ma - jes -
fall, We at His feet may fall! We'll join the e - ver -

(refrain)

di - a - dem,
by His grace,
at His feet, And crown   Him,
ty as - cribe,
last - ing song, crown Him, crown Him, crown Him, crown Him

crown

crown Him, crown Him, crown Him, And crown Him Lord of all. A - men.

Him.

48   Alleluia! Sing to Jesus!

Hallelujah! For the Lord our God the Almighty reigns/Rev 19:6

William Dix

Rowland Prichard
harm Ralph Vaughan Williams; des Betty Pulkingham
Hyfrydol

Verse 1: ia! Al - le - lu - ia! Al-le-lu - ia! Al - le - lu - ia! Al - - - le - lu - ia! Al - le - lu - - ia!

Verse 2: Zi - on Thun - der like a migh - ty flood; Je - sus out of ev - 'ry na - tion Hath re - deemed us by his blood.

Verse 3: ceived him, When the for - ty days were o'er, Shall our hearts for - get his prom - ise, 'I am with you ev - er more?'

Verse 4: sin - ners, Earth's re - deem - er, plead for me, Where the songs of all the sin - less Sweep a - cross the crys - tal sea.

4. Alleluia! King eternal,
    Thee the Lord of lords we own:
Alleluia! born of Mary,
    Earth Thy footstool, heav'n Thy throne:
Thou within the veil hast entered,
    Robed in flesh, our great high priest:
Thou on earth both priest and victim
    In the eucharistic feast.

5. Alleluia! sing to Jesus!
    His the scepter, His the throne;
Alleluia! His the triumph,
    His the victory alone;
Hark! the songs of holy Zion
    Thunder like a mighty flood;
Jesus out of every nation
    Hath redeemed us by His blood.

49 Sing Alleluia

Jesus is Lord/1 Cor 12:3

Source unknown   *Source unknown*

 C   Em   Am
1. Men: Sing alleluia to the Lord;
           Women: Sing alleluia to the Lord;
    C   G   E
Men: Sing alleluia to the Lord;
        Women: Sing allelu-ia;
  Am   G   Dm   Em
Men: Sing alleluia; sing alleluia;
Women: Al–   le– lu–   ia;
     C   Em   Am
Unison: Sing alleluia to the Lord.

2. Jesus is Lord of heaven and earth....

3. Jesus is King and Lord of all....

4. He's coming back to claim His own....

50 Redeemed

In him we have redemption through his blood/Eph 1:7

Fanny J Crosby   *A L Butler*

1. Re-deemed, how I love to pro-claim it! Re-deemed, by the blood of the Lamb; Re-deemed thro' His in-fi-nite mer-cy, His
2. Re-deemed, and so hap-py in Je-sus, No lan-guage my rap-ture can tell; I know that the light of His pres-ence With
3. I think of my bless-ed Re-deem-er, I think of Him all the day long; I sing, for I can-not be si-lent; His

child, and for - ev - er, I am.
me doth con - tin - ual - ly dwell.
love is the theme of my song.

Re - deemed, re - deemed, Re -

deemed by the blood of the Lamb;

Re - deemed, how I

love to pro - claim it! His child and for - ev - er I am.

51   Now unto the King Eternal

Praise & Worship

To the King of ages . . . be honor and glory for ever and ever. Amen./
1 Tim 1:17

1 Timothy 1:17

Lorraine Sonnenberg

F
Now unto the King eternal, immortal, invisible,
     C7   F   C7   C7   F
The only wise God, the only wise God,
C9 F   C7   F   C7
Be honor and glory for ever and ever. Amen. Amen.
   F   C7   F
Be honor and glory for ever and ever. Amen.

Who is a God like thee, pardoning iniquity . . . ?/Mic 7:18

Samuel Davies   *John Newton*
                                                              Sovereignty

1. Great God of won - ders! all Thy ways Are match-less, God - like,
2. In won-der lost, with trem-bling joy We take the par - don
3. O may this strange, this match-less grace, This God - like mir - a -

and di - vine; But the fair glo - ries of Thy grace More God-like
of our God; Par - don for crimes of deep - est dye, A par-don
cle of love, Fill the whole earth with grate - ful praise, And all th'an -

and un - ri -valed shine, More God-like and un - ri -valed shine.
bought with Je - sus' blood; A par -don bought with Je - sus' blood:
gel - ic choirs a - bove, And all th'an - gel - ic choirs a -bove.

Refrain

Who is a par-d'ning God like Thee? Or who has grace so

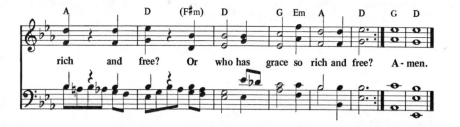

rich   and   free?   Or   who has   grace so   rich and free?   A - men.

53   I Cannot Tell Why He

Praise & Worship

But when the time had fully come, God sent forth his Son/Gal 4:4

William Y Fullerton

Traditional Irish melody
Londonderry Air

G   C   C7   F
1. I cannot tell why He whom angels worship
       G   C   Am   G7
   Should set His love upon the sons of men,
       C   C7   F
Or, why, as Shepherd, He should seek the wanderers,
         C/G   G7   C
   To bring them back, they know not how or when:
   G7   C   F   C
But this I know, that He was born of Mary,
       G7   Am   C/G   Dm
   When Bethlehem's manger was His only home,
G7   C   F   C/G
And that He lived at Nazareth and labored,
     D7   Fm   C/G   G7   C
   And so the Savior, Savior of the world is come.

2. I cannot tell how silently He suffered,
   As with His peace He graced this place of tears,
Or how His heart upon the cross was broken,
   The crown of pain to three and thirty years:
But this I know, He heals the broken hearted,
   And stays our sin and calms our lurking fear,
And lifts the burden from the heavy-laden,
   For yet the Savior, Savior of the world is here.

3. I cannot tell how He will win the nations,
   How He will claim His earthly heritage,
How satisfy the needs and aspirations
   Of East and West, of sinner and of sage:
But this I know, all flesh shall see His glory,
   And He shall reap the harvest He has sown,
And some glad day His sun shall shine in splendor
   When He the Savior, Savior of the world is known.

4. I cannot tell how all the lands shall worship,
   When at His bidding every storm is stilled,
Or who can say how great the jubilation
   When all the hearts of men with love are filled:
But this I know, the skies will thrill with gladness,
   And myriad, myriad human voices sing,
And earth to heaven, and heaven to earth will answer,
   At last the Savior, Savior of the world is King!

by permission of the Psalms & Hymns Trust, London.

Looking to Jesus the pioneer and perfecter of our faith/Heb 12:2

Ray Palmer   *Lowell Mason*
                                                                Olivet

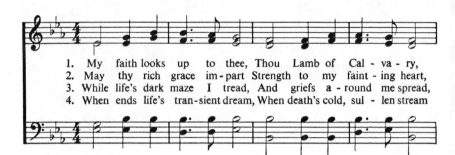

1. My faith looks up to thee, Thou Lamb of Cal - va - ry,
2. May thy rich grace im - part Strength to my faint - ing heart,
3. While life's dark maze I tread, And griefs a - round me spread,
4. When ends life's tran-sient dream, When death's cold, sul - len stream

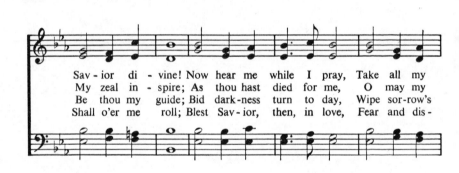

Sav - ior di - vine! Now hear me while I pray, Take all my
My zeal in - spire; As thou hast died for me, O may my
Be thou my guide; Bid dark-ness turn to day, Wipe sor-row's
Shall o'er me roll; Blest Sav - ior, then, in love, Fear and dis -

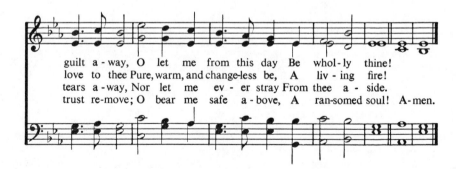

guilt a - way, O let me from this day Be whol-ly thine!
love to thee Pure, warm, and change-less be, A liv - ing fire!
tears a - way, Nor let me ev - er stray From thee a - side.
trust re-move; O bear me safe a - bove, A ran-somed soul! A - men.

55 Amazing Grace

The grace of that one man Jesus Christ abounded for many/Rom 5:15

John Newton
stanza 6 anon

Traditional American melody

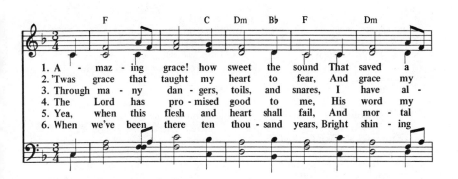

1. A - maz - ing grace! how sweet the sound That saved a
2. 'Twas grace that taught my heart to fear, And grace my
3. Through ma - ny dan - gers, toils, and snares, I have al -
4. The Lord has pro - mised good to me, His word my
5. Yea, when this flesh and heart shall fail, And mor - tal
6. When we've been there ten thou - sand years, Bright shin - ing

wretch like me! I once was lost, but now am
fears re - lieved; How pre - cious did that grace ap -
read - y come; 'Tis grace hath brought me safe thus
hope se - cures; He will my shield and por - tion
life shall cease, I shall pos - sess with - in the
as the sun, We've no less days to sing God's

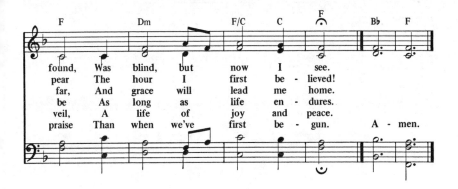

found, Was blind, but now I see.
pear The hour I first be - lieved!
far, And grace will lead me home.
be As long as life en - dures.
veil, A life of joy and peace.
praise Than when we've first be - gun. A - men.

56   What a Friend We Have in Jesus   Praise & Worship

In Christ . . . we have boldness and confidence of access through our faith in him/Eph 3:11-12

Joseph M Scriven

1. What a Friend we have in Jesus
   All our sins and griefs to bear!
What a privilege to carry
   Everything to God in prayer!
O what peace we often forfeit,
   O what needless pain we bear,
All because we do not carry
   Everything to God in prayer!

2. Have we trials and temptations?
   Is there trouble anywhere?
We should never be discouraged:
   Take it to the Lord in prayer.

Can we find a friend so faithful,
   Who will all our sorrows share?
Jesus knows our every weakness:
   Take it to the Lord in prayer.

3. Are we weak and heavy-laden,
   Cumbered with a load of care?
Jesus only is our refuge:
   Take it to the Lord in prayer.
Do thy friends despise, forsake thee?
   Take it to the Lord in prayer;
In His arms He'll take and shield thee!
   Thou wilt find a solace there. Amen.

57   To God Be the Glory   Praise & Worship
My Tribute

Not to us, O LORD, not to us, but to thy name give glory/Ps 115:1

Andraé Crouch

Andraé Crouch
My Tribute

To God be the glo - ry; to God be the glo - ry; to

God be the glo - ry for the things He has done. With His

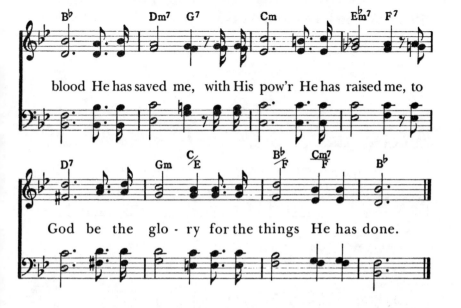

blood He has saved me, with His pow'r He has raised me, to

God be the glo - ry for the things He has done.

58 Crown Him with Many Crowns

Praise & Worship

On his head are many diadems/Rev 19:12

Matthew Bridges
stanza 2 Godfrey Thring

George Elvey
Diademata

1. Crown Him with many crowns,
   The Lamb upon His throne;
   Hark! how the heavenly anthem drowns
   All music but its own.
   Awake, my soul, and sing
   Of Him who died for thee,
   And hail Him as thy matchless King
   Through all eternity.

2. Crown Him the Lord of life,
   Who triumphed o'er the grave;
   And rose victorious in the strife
   For those He came to save;
   His glories now we sing,
   Who died and rose on high,
   Who died eternal life to bring,
   And lives, that death may die.

3. Crown Him the Lord of peace,
   Whose pow'r a scepter sways
   From pole to pole that wars may cease,
   And all be prayer and praise:
   His reign shall know no end,
   And round His pierced feet
   Fair flowers of paradise extend
   Their fragrance ever sweet.

4. Crown Him the Lord of love;
   Behold His hands and side,
   Those wounds yet visible above,
   In beauty glorified:
   All hail, Redeemer, hail!
   For Thou hast died for me:
   Thy praise and glory shall not fail
   Throughout eternity. Amen.

For God so loved the world that he gave his only Son/Jn 3:16

John 3:16-17

John Stainer
Stainer

God so loved the world, God so loved the world,

that He gave His on - ly be - got - ten Son, that who - so be -

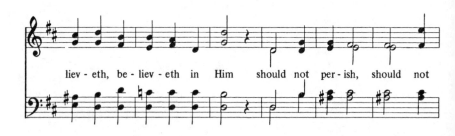

liev - eth, be - liev - eth in Him should not per - ish, should not

per - ish but have ev - er - last - ing life. For God sent not His

Clap Your Hands

Clap your hands, all peoples/Ps 47:1

Jimmy Owens   *Jimmy Owens*

Clap your hands, all you peo - ple, Shout un - to God with a voice of tri - umph,

Clap your hands, all you peo - ple, Shout un - to God with a voice of praise! Ho -

san - na, ho - san - na, Shout un - to God with a voice of tri - umph,

Praise Him, praise Him, Shout un - to God with a voice of praise!

61   ## Our Father

The Lord's Prayer

Our Father who art in heaven, Hallowed be thy name/Mt 6:9

Matthew 6:9-13   *West Indian melody*
Versified by compilers of Praise Ways   *arr compilers of* Praise Ways

1. Our   Fath - er,   Who art   in   hea - ven,
2. On   the earth as   it is   in   hea - ven,
3. give   us   all   our   tres - pass - es,
4. lead   us   not   in   -   to   temp - ta - tion,
5. Thine is   the king-dom, the power and the glo - ry,
6. men,   A - men, A - men,   A - men,

The words "Hallowed be Thy Name" are sung after every two bars.

62 Now unto Him Who Is Able

Jude Benediction

To the only God . . . be glory, majesty, dominion, and authority/Jude 25

Jude 24-25

Olive Wood

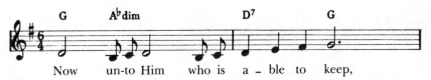

Now un-to Him who is a – ble to keep,

a- ble to keep you from fall — ing,

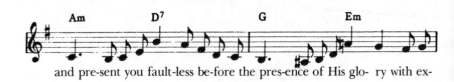

and pre-sent you fault-less be-fore the pres-ence of His glo- ry with ex-

ceed — ing joy, To the on- ly wise God our

Sav — iour, be glo-ry and ma- jes- ty, do-

min – ion and power, both now and for- ev- er. A ——— men.

63 The Love of God

Praise & Worship

Who shall separate us from the love of Christ?/Rom 8:35

F M Lehman   *F M Lehman*

1. The love of God is great-er far Than tongue or
2. When years of time shall pass a - way, And earth-ly
3. Could we with ink the o - cean fill, And were the

pen can ev - er tell; It goes be - yond the high - est
thrones and king-doms fall, When men, who here re - fuse to
skies of parch-ment made, Were ev - ery stalk on earth a

star, And reach - es to the low - est hell; The guilt - y
pray, On rocks and hills and moun-tains call, God's love so
quill, And ev - 'ry man a scribe by trade, To write the

pair bowed down with care, God gave His Son to win;
sure, shall still en - dure, All mea - sure - less and strong;
love of God a - bove Would drain the o - cean dry.

His err - ing child He rec - on - ciled, and par - doned from his sin.
Re-deem-ing grace to A-dam's race the saints' and an - gels' song.
Nor could the scroll con - tain the whole, Though stretched from sky to sky.

O love of God, how rich and pure! How mea-sure-less and

strong! It shall for ev - er-more en - dure The saints' and an - gels' song.

He always lives to make intercession for them/Heb 7:25

Charles Wesley *Traditional American melody*

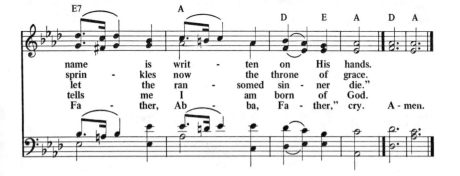

name	is	writ - ten	on	His	hands.
sprin -	kles	now	the	throne	of	grace.
let	the	ran -	somed	sin -	ner	die."
tells	me	I	am	born	of	God.
Fa -	ther,	Ab -	ba,	Fa -	ther,"	cry.	A - men.

65   For Those Tears I Died

Praise & Worship

Come, let him who desires take the water of life without price/Rev 22:17

Marsha J Stevens   *Marsha J Stevens*

    E   C#m   A   B
1. You said You'd come and share all my sorrows.
    E   C#m   A   B
You said You'd be there for all my tomorrows.
    E   B   A   B
I came so close to sending You away,
      E   C#m   A   B
But just like You promised You came there to stay,
     B7   E E7
   I just had to pray.

Refrain
          A   E
And Jesus said, "Come to the water, stand by My side.
 B   E E7
I know you are thirsty, you won't be denied.
    A   E
I felt every tear drop when in darkness you cried,
     B   B7   E
And I strove to remind you that for those tears I died."

2. Your goodness so great I can't understand.
And, dear Lord, I know that all this was planned.
I know You're here now and always will be
Your love loosed my chains and in You I'm free.
   But Jesus, why me?

3. Jesus, I give You my heart and my soul.
I know now without God I'd never be whole.
Savior, You opened all the right doors,
And I thank You and praise You from earth's humble shores.
   Take me, I'm Yours.

66 Unbounded Grace

Praise & Worship

God is able to provide you with every blessing in abundance/2 Cor 9:8

John E Walvoord

Don Wyrtzen

1. Un - bound - ed grace— it reached to me When hope was
2. Grace was for me the on - ly way My guilt could
3. God's grace does not on me de - pend— It's God who
4. The u - ni - verse with joy will ring When grace has

gone from view; In my de - spair, Christ came to
find re - lief; My des - ti - ny was changed that
is my Stay; His love is of - fered with - out
won the day; As all cre - a - tion joins to

me As He a - lone could do.
day I reached out in be - lief.
end, He walks with me each day.
sing, "Praise God, who paid the

way!" Un - bound - ed grace! A - maz - ing grace!

Thou Art Worthy

Praise & Worship

Worthy art thou, our Lord and God, to receive glory and honor and power/Rev 4:11

Revelation 4:11

Pauline Michael Mills

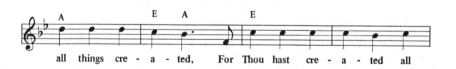

68 Rejoice in the Lord Always

Rejoice in the Lord always; again I will say, Rejoice/Phil 4:4

Philippians 4:4

Traditional round

```
1.  F                 Gm  C7     F
Rejoice in the Lord always, again I say, rejoice!
2.  F                 Gm  C7     F
Rejoice in the Lord always, again I say, rejoice!
3.  F       Gm  C7    F
Rejoice, rejoice, again I say, rejoice!
4.  F       Gm  C7    F
Rejoice, rejoice, again I say, rejoice!
```

69 Holy, Holy

Holy, holy, holy, is the Lord God Almighty/Rev 4:8

Jimmy Owens   *Jimmy Owens*

(Unison) 1. Ho - ly, ho - ly, ho - ly, ho - ly. Ho - ly, ho - ly,_____ Lord God Al - migh - ty; And we lift our hearts be-fore you as a

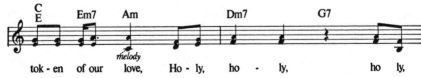

tok - en of our love, Ho - ly, ho - ly, ho ly,

ho - ly.   2. Gra - cious   lu   jah.

Any of the following may be sung in parts:

2. Gracious Father, gracious Father,
We're so glad to be Your children, gracious Father;
And we lift our heads before You as a token of our love,
   Gracious Father, gracious Father.

3. Precious Jesus, precious Jesus,
We're so glad that You've redeemed us, precious Jesus,
And we lift our hands before You as a token of our love,
   Precious Jesus, precious Jesus.

4. Holy Spirit, Holy Spirit,
Come and fill our hearts anew, Holy Spirit,
And we lift our voice before You as a token of our love,
   Holy Spirit, Holy Spirit.

5. Holy, holy, holy, holy.
Holy, holy, Lord God Almighty;
And we lift our hearts before You as a token of our love,
   Holy, holy, holy, holy.

6. Hallelujah, hallelujah,
Hallelujah, hallelujah,
And we lift our hearts before You as a token of our love,
   Hallelujah, hallelujah.

70   Great Is the Lord   Praise & Worship

Great is the LORD and greatly to be praised/Ps 48:1

Psalm 48:1-2   *Traditional*

    C   G7
Great is the Lord, and greatly to be praised
                                    C
In the city of our God, in the mountain of His holiness.
                          C7   F
Beautiful for situation, the joy of the whole earth,
                   C   F   G7   C
Is Mount Zion, on the sides of the north, the city of the great King.

Christ died for our sins, . . . was buried, . . . was raised/1 Cor 15:3-4

Traditional   *Traditional*

Chorus:	Come and	praise	the	Lord	our	King,	Hal - le - lu - jah!
1.	Christ was	born	in	Beth - le -	hem,	Hal - le - lu - jah!
2.	He grew	up	an	earth - ly	child,	Hal - le - lu - jah!
3.	Je - sus	died	at	Cal - va -	ry,	Hal - le - lu - jah!
4.	He will	cleanse	us	from our	sin,	Hal - le - lu - jah!
5.	We will	live	with	Him some	day,	Hal - le - lu - jah!

Come and	praise	the	Lord	our	King,	Hal - le - lu - jah!
Son of	God	and	Son	of	Man,	Hal - le - lu - jah!
Of the	world	but	un -	de -	filed,	Hal - le - lu - jah!
Rose a -	gain	tri -	um -	phant -	ly,	Hal - le - lu - jah!
If we	live	by	faith	in	Him,	Hal - le - lu - jah!
And for -	ev -	er	with	Him	stay,	Hal - le - lu - jah!

72 **Let's Enjoy God Together**   Praise & Worship

Missionary Communion Hymn

We who are many are one body, for we all partake of the
one bread/1 Cor 10:17

Margaret Clarkson   *Tedd Smith*

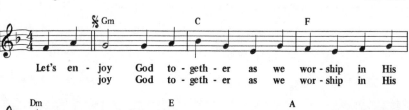

| Let's en - joy | God | to - geth - er | as | we | wor - ship | in | His |
| joy | God | to - geth - er | as | we | wor - ship | in | His |

| pres - ence; | He | is | here, | as | He | pro - mised, | for | we |
| pres - ence; | One | in | praise, | one | in | pur - pose, | one | in |

Surely I am coming soon/Rev 22:20

Frances R Havergal

William H Monk
Beverley

1. Thou art com - ing, O my Sa - vior, Thou art com - ing,
2. Thou art com - ing, Thou art com - ing; We shall meet Thee
3. Thou art com - ing; at Thy Ta - ble We are wit - ness -
4. O the joy to see Thee reign - ing, Thee, my own be -

O my King, In Thy beau - ty all re - splen - dent, In Thy glo - ry
on Thy way, We shall see Thee, we shall know Thee, We shall bless Thee,
es for this; While re - mem - b'ring hearts Thou meet - est In com - mun - ion
lov - ed Lord! E - v'ry tongue Thy Name con - fes - sing, Wor - ship, hon - or,

all tran - scen - dent; Well may we re - joice and sing: Com - ing! in the
we shall show Thee All our hearts could ne - ver say: What an an - them
clear - est, sweet - est, Earn - est of our com - ing bliss, Show - ing not Thy
glo - ry, bles - sing Brought to Thee with glad ac - cord; Thee, my Mas - ter

open - ing east Her - ald bright - ness slow - ly swells; Com - ing!
that will be, Ring - ing out our love to Thee, Pour - ing
death a - lone, And Thy love ex - ceed - ing great, But Thy
and my Friend, Vin - di - cat - ed and en - throned; Un - to

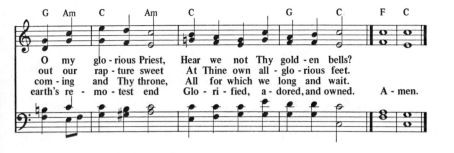

O my glo-rious Priest, Hear we not Thy gold-en bells?
out our rap-ture sweet At Thine own all-glo-rious feet.
com-ing and Thy throne, All for which we long and wait.
earth's re-mo-test end Glo-ri-fied, a-dored, and owned. A-men.

74 "Man of Sorrows"

Praise & Worship

The Son of Man will appear ... to gather his chosen/Mt 23:30-31

Philip Bliss

Philip Bliss
Man of Sorrows

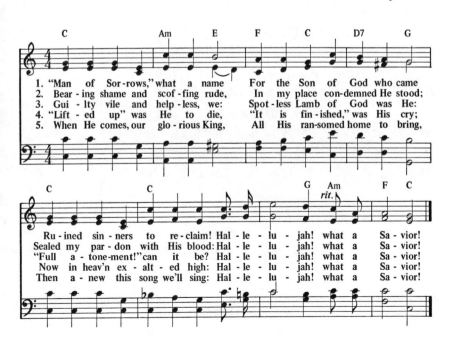

1. "Man of Sor-rows," what a name For the Son of God who came
2. Bear-ing shame and scof-fing rude, In my place con-demned He stood;
3. Gui-lty vile and help-less, we: Spot-less Lamb of God was He:
4. "Lift-ed up" was He to die, "It is fin-ished," was His cry;
5. When He comes, our glo-rious King, All His ran-somed home to bring,

Ru-ined sin-ners to re-claim! Hal-le-lu-jah! what a Sa-vior!
Sealed my par-don with His blood: Hal-le-lu-jah! what a Sa-vior!
"Full a-tone-ment!" can it be? Hal-le-lu-jah! what a Sa-vior!
Now in heav'n ex-alt-ed high: Hal-le-lu-jah! what a Sa-vior!
Then a-new this song we'll sing: Hal-le-lu-jah! what a Sa-vior!

PART II

COMMITMENT & SERVICE

Who is on the Lord's side?
Who will serve the King?
Who will be His helpers
Other lives to bring?
Who will leave the world's side?
Who will face the foe?
Who is on the Lord's side?
Who for Him will go?

By Thy call of mercy,
By Thy grace divine,
We are on the Lord's side,
Savior, we are Thine.

Francis R Havergal

This . . . shall be to me a name of joy, a praise and a glory before all the nations/Jer 33:9

Bryan J Leech

Paul Liljestrand
Conrad

1. Thro' all the world let ev-ery na-tion sing to God the King,
2. Thro' all the world let ev-ery man ex-press true right-eous-ness,
3. Thro' all the world let ev-ery man em-brace the gift of grace,
4. If all the world in ev-ery part shall hear, and God re-vere,

As Lord may Christ pre-side where now He is de-fied,
May Christ now be the norm to which all men con-form,
May Christ's great light con-sume our dark-est cit-ies' gloom,
We must be moved to care, and in His name to share

And sov-'reign place His throne in lands not yet His own.
His pas-sion cure the sin that fes-ters from with-in.
May Christ's great love ef-face hos-til-i-ties of race.
The lib-er-a-ting word which must be told a-broad.

Thro' all the world let ev-ery na-tion sing to God the King.
Thro' all the world let ev-ery man ex-press true right-eous-ness.
Thro' all the world let ev-ery man em-brace the gift of grace.
Then all the world in ev-ery part shall hear, and God re-vere.

Who Is on the Lord's Side?

Who is on the LORD's side?/Ex 32:26

Frances R Havergal

Caradog Roberts
Rachie

1. Who is on the Lord's side? Who will serve the King? Who will
2. Not for weight of glo - ry, Not for crown and palm, En - ter
3. Je - sus, Thou has bought us, Not with gold or gem, But with
4. Fierce may be the con - flict, Strong may be the foe, But the

be His hel - pers Oth - er lives to bring? Who will leave the world's side?
we the ar - my, Raise the war - rior psalm; But for love that claim - eth
Thine own life blood, For Thy di - a - dem. With Thy bles - sing fil - ling
King's own ar - my, None can o - ver - throw. Round His stand- ard rang - ing

Who will face the foe? Who is on the Lord's side? Who for Him will
Lives for whom He died; He whom Je - sus nam- eth Must be on His
Each who comes to Thee, Thou has made us wil - ling, Thou has made us
Vic - t'ry is se - cure; For His truth un - chang-ing Makes the tri - umph

go? By Thy call of mer - cy, By Thy grace di - vine,
side. By Thy love con-strain - ing, By Thy grace di - vine,
free. By Thy grand re - demp - tion, By Thy grace di - vine,
sure. Joy - ful - ly en - list - ing, By Thy grace di - vine,

By Thy call of mer - cy By Thy grace di - vine

We are on the Lord's side, Sa - vior, we are Thine. A - men.

77 We Have Heard the Joyful Sound Commitment & Service

All the ends of the earth shall see the salvation of . . . God/Is 52:10

Pricilla J Owens

Josiah Booth
Limpsfield

1. We have heard the joy - ful sound; Je - sus saves! Spread the glad - ness
all a - round; Je - sus saves! Bear the news to e - v'ry land, Climb the
steeps and cross the waves; On - ward! 'tis the Lord's com - mand: Je - sus saves!

2. Sing a - bove the bat - tle strife; Je - sus saves! By His death and
end - less life, Je - sus saves! Sing it soft - ly through the gloom, When the
heart for mer - cy craves; Sing in tri - umph o'er the tomb: Je - sus saves!

3. Give the winds a might - y voice: Je - sus saves! Let the na - tions
now re - joice: Je - sus saves! Sing ye is - lands of the sea; E - cho
back ye o - cean caves; Shout sal - va - tion full and free: Je - sus saves!

music: from the Church Hymnary *by permission of Oxford University Press.*

I came that they may have life, and have it abundantly/Jn 10:10

Billie Hanks, Jr   *Billie Hanks, Jr*

1. ___ Lone-ly voic-es cry-ing in the cit-y, ___ Lone-ly voic-es
2. ___ Lone-ly fac-es look-ing for the sun-rise ___ Just to find an-
3. ___ Lone-ly eyes, I see them in the sub-way; ___ Bur-dened by the
4. A-bun-dant life He came to tru-ly give man; ___ But so few His

sound-ing like a child. ___ Lone-ly voic-es come from bus-y peo-ple;
oth-er bus-y day. ___ Lone-ly fac-es all a-round the cit-y; ___
wor-ries of the day: ___ Men at lei-sure, but they're so un-hap-py,
gift of grace re-ceive. ___ Lone-ly peo-ple live in ev-ery cit-y;

___ Too dis-turbed to stop a lit-tle while. ___ Lone-ly voic-es ___
___ Men a-fraid, but too a-shamed to pray. ___ Lone-ly fac-es ___
___ Tired of fool-ish roles they try to play. ___ Lone-ly peo-ple ___
___ Men who face a dark and lone-ly grave. ___ Lone-ly fac-es ___

___ fill my dreams: ___ Lone-ly voic-es ___ haunt my mem-o-ry. ___
___ do I see; ___ Lone-ly fac-es ___ haunt my mem-o-ry. ___
___ do I see; ___ Lone-ly peo-ple ___ haunt my mem-o-ry. ___
___ do I see; ___ Lone-ly voic-es ___ call-ing out to me. ___

79 **Seek Ye First the Kingdom of God** Commitment & Service

Seek first his kingdom and his righteousness/Mt 6:33

Matthew 6:33; 4:4; 7:7; 11:28; Luke 9:23

Source unknown
des Karen Lafferty

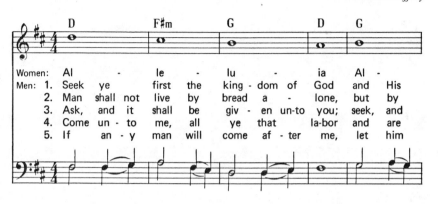

Women: Al - le - lu - ia Al -
Men: 1. Seek ye first the king - dom of God and His
2. Man shall not live by bread a - lone, but by
3. Ask, and it shall be giv - en un-to you; seek, and
4. Come un - to me, all ye that la-bor and are
5. If an - y man will come af - ter me, let him

Women: le - lu - Al - le -
Men: right - eous - ness, and all these things shall be
eve - ry word that pro - ceeds from the
ye shall find; knock, and the door shall be
heav - y la - den, and I will give sweet
de - ny him-self, take up his cross and

Women: lu - ia Al - le - lu - ia.
Men: add - ed un - to you. Al - le - lu, al - le - lu - ia.
mouth of God. Al - le - lu, al - le - lu - ia.
o - pened un - to you. Al - le - lu, al - le - lu - ia.
rest un - to your souls. Al - le - lu, al - le - lu - ia.
dai - ly fol - low me. Al - le - lu, al - le - lu - ia.

We have received grace . . . to bring about the obedience of faith for the sake of his name among all the nations/Rom 1:5

Margaret Clarkson

Donald P Hustad
Delta

1. Pro - claim the Sav - ior's name, All we who know His grace; Let ev - 'ry heart leap high with joy To sound His praise! Pro - claim His ris - en life, His glo - ries blaze a - broad, That
2. Pro - claim Him Son of God, Cre - a - tor of the spheres. The Son of Man who wept for man With hu - man tears; Who laid His glo - ry by To die man's death for men, Who

4. O live your life in me, My Sav - ior, Mas - ter, King, Till all my be - ing crown with truth The praise I bring! Show forth in me Your pow'r To cleanse and make men new, That

Present your bodies as a living sacrifice, holy and acceptable
to God/Rom 12:1

Frances R Havergal

Wolfgang Amadeus Mozart
Nottingham

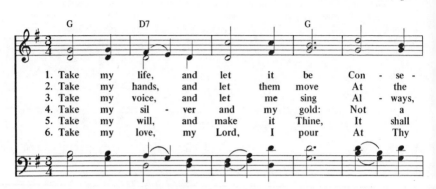

1. Take my life, and let it be Con - se -
2. Take my hands, and let them move At the
3. Take my voice, and let me sing Al - ways,
4. Take my sil - ver and my gold: Not a
5. Take my will, and make it Thine, It shall
6. Take my love, my Lord, I pour At Thy

crat - ed, Lord, to Thee; Take my mo - ments and my
im - pulse of Thy love; Take my feet, and let them
on - ly, for my King; Take my lips, and let them
mite would I with - hold; Take my in - tel - lect, and
be no long - er mine; Take my heart, it is Thine
feet its trea - sure store; Take my - self, and I will

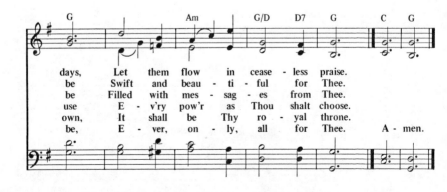

days, Let them flow in cease - less praise.
be Swift and beau - ti - ful for Thee.
be Filled with mes - sag - es from Thee.
use E - v'ry pow'r as Thou shalt choose.
own, It shall be Thy ro - yal throne.
be, E - ver, on - ly, all for Thee. A - men.

I Will Instruct Thee   Commitment & Service

I will instruct you and teach you the way you should go/Ps 32:8

Psalm 32:8   *Marlene D Washington*

I will in - struct thee   and teach thee in   the   way which thou shalt

go: I   will guide   thee   with   mine   eye.   I   will in -

struct thee   and teach thee   in   the   way which thou shalt go: I   will

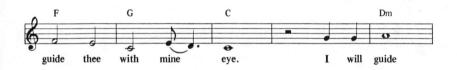

guide   thee   with   mine   eye.   I   will guide

thee,   I   will guide   thee,   I   will guide   thee

with   mine   eye.   I   will guide   thee,   I   will

guide   thee,   I   will guide   thee   with   mine   eye.

And Jesus said to them, "Follow me"/Mk 1:17

Source unknown   *Traditional*

C
1. I have decided to follow Jesus,
C7   F   C
I have decided to follow Jesus,

I have decided to follow Jesus,
                   G7
No turning back, No turning back.

2. The world behind me, the cross before me;
The world behind me, the cross before me;
The world behind me, the cross before me;
No turning back, No turning back.

3. Tho' none go with me, I still will
   follow,
Tho' none go with me, I still will follow,
Tho' none go with me, I still will follow,
No turning back, No turning back.

4. Will you decide now to follow Jesus?
Will you decide now to follow Jesus?
Will you decide now to follow Jesus?
No turning back, No turning back.

I was thirsty and you gave me drink/Mt 25:35

Frank Mason North   *Traditional American melody*

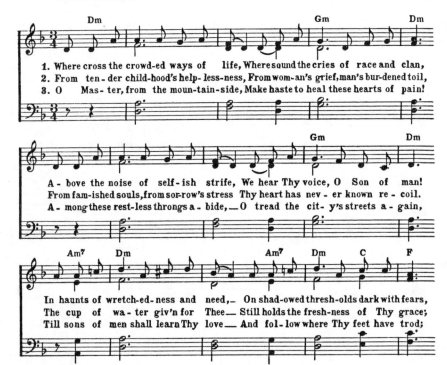

1. Where cross the crowd-ed ways of life, Where sound the cries of race and clan,
2. From ten-der child-hood's help-less-ness, From wom-an's grief, man's bur-dened toil,
3. O   Mas-ter, from the moun-tain-side, Make haste to heal these hearts of pain!

A-bove the noise of self-ish strife, We hear Thy voice, O Son of man!
From fam-ished souls, from sor-row's stress Thy heart has nev-er known re-coil.
A-mong these rest-less throngs a-bide,— O tread the cit-y's streets a-gain,

In haunts of wretch-ed-ness and need,— On shad-owed thresh-olds dark with fears,
The cup of wa-ter giv'n for Thee— Still holds the fresh-ness of Thy grace;
Till sons of men shall learn Thy love— And fol-low where Thy feet have trod;

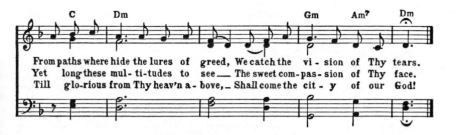

From paths where hide the lures of greed, We catch the vi-sion of Thy tears.
Yet long these mul-ti-tudes to see— The sweet com-pas-sion of Thy face.
Till glo-rious from Thy heav'n a-bove,— Shall come the cit-y of our God!

85 When I Survey

Commitment & Service

Far be it from me to glory except in the cross/Gal 6:14

Isaac Watts

Tune of Hymn 84

1. When I survey the wondrous cross
On which the Prince of glory died,
My richest gain I count but loss,
And pour contempt on all my pride.

2. Forbid it, Lord, that I should boast,
Save in the death of Christ, my God;
All the vain things that charm me most,
I sacrifice them to His blood.

3. See, from His head, His hands, His feet,
Sorrow and love flow mingled down;
Did e'er such love and sorrow meet,
Or thorns compose so rich a crown?

4. Were the whole realm of nature mine,
That were a present far too small;
Love so amazing, so divine,
Demands my soul, my life, my all. Amen.

86 I Heard the Voice of Jesus Say

Commitment & Service

Come to me, all who labor . . . and I will give you rest/Mt 11:28

Horatius Bonar

John B Dykes
Vox Dilecti

1. I heard the voice of Jesus say,
"Come unto Me and rest;
Lay down, thou weary one, lay down
Thy head upon My breast."
I came to Jesus as I was,
Weary, and worn, and sad;
I found in Him a resting place,
And He has made me glad.

2. I heard the voice of Jesus say,
"Behold, I freely give
The living water; thirsty one,
Stoop down, and drink, and live."
I came to Jesus, and I drank
Of that life-giving stream;
My thirst was quenched, my soul revived,
And now I live in Him.

3. I heard the voice of Jesus say,
"I am this dark world's Light;
Look unto Me, thy morn shall rise,
And all thy day be bright."
I looked to Jesus, and I found
In Him my Star, my Sun;
And in that Light of life I'll walk,
Till traveling days are done. Amen.

The creation waits with eager longing for the revealing of the sons
of God/Rom 8:19

Margaret Clarkson

Margaret Clarkson
York Downs

1. Lord of the U - ni - verse, Hope of the world, Lord of the li - mit - less
2. Lord of the U - ni - verse, Hope of the world, Lord of the in - fi - nite,
3. Lord of the U - ni - verse, Hope of the world, Send out Your light to the
4. Lord of the U - ni - verse, Hope of the world, How Your cre - a - tion cries

reach - es of space, Here on this pla - net You put on our flesh,
e - ons of time, You came a - mong us, lived our brief years,
ends of the earth; May we who know You o - bey Your com - mand,
out for re - lease! Looks for You, longs for You, wat - ches and waits,

Vast-ness con-fined in the womb of a maid, Born in our like - ness you
Tas - ted our griefs, our a - lone-ness, our fears, Con-quered our death, made e
Go with the grace of Your gos - pel to all, Bring-ing sal - va - tion and
Prays for Your king-dom of jus - tice and peace! Mak - er, Re-deem - er, Tri -

ran - somed our race:
ter - ni - ty ours:
free - dom and joy: Sa - vior, we wor - ship You, praise and a - dore,
um - phant One, come!

Help us to hon-or You more and yet more, Help us to hon-or You more and yet more!

88 O Breath of Life

Commitment & Service

Wilt thou not revive us again . . . ?/Ps 85:6

Bessie P Head

Mary J Hammond
Spiritus Vitae

1. O Breath of Life, come sweep-ing through us, Re - vive Thy
2. O Wind of God, come bend us, break us, Till hum - bly
3. O Breath of Love, come breathe with - in us, Re - new - ing
4. Re - vive us, Lord! Is zeal a - bat - ing While har - vest

church with life and pow'r; O Breath of Life, come, cleanse, re -
we con - fess our need; Then in Thy ten - der - ness re -
thought and will and heart; Come, Love of Christ, a - fresh to
fields are vast and white? Re - vive us, Lord, the world is

new us, And fit Thy church to meet this hour.
make us, Re - vive, re - store, for this we plead.
win us, Re - vive Thy church in e - v'ry part.
wait - ing, E - quip Thy church to spread the light. A - men.

For God So Loved People

We preach Christ crucified/1 Cor 1:23

Beatrice Bush Bixler

Beatrice Bush Bixler

For God so lov'd peo-ple He gave His on-ly Son. Let it

ring from ev-'ry stee-ple, Let it be on ev-'ry tongue that

God so lov'd peo-ple, He en-ter'd Time and Space For

those of ev-'ry lan-guage, For those of ev-'ry race. Since

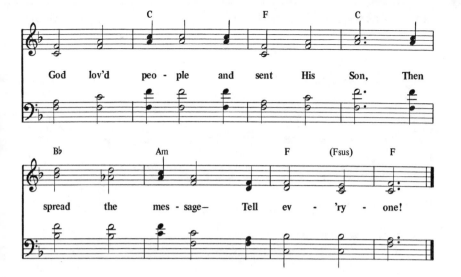

90 Lord, in the Fullness of My Might Commitment & Service

Be strong and of good courage . . . do according to all the law/Josh 1:6-7

Thomas H Gill

C E Miller
Es Ist Ein Born

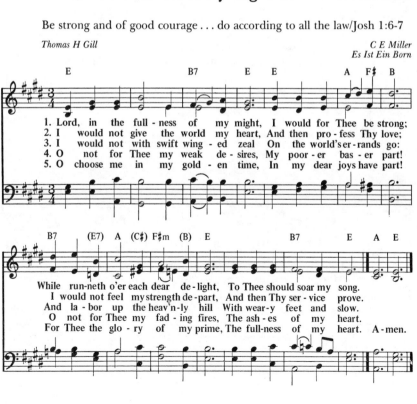

1. Lord, in the full - ness of my might, I would for Thee be strong;
2. I would not give the world my heart, And then pro - fess Thy love;
3. I would not with swift wing - ed zeal On the world's er - rands go:
4. O not for Thee my weak de - sires, My poor - er bas - er part!
5. O choose me in my gold - en time, In my dear joys have part!

While run - neth o'er each dear de - light, To Thee should soar my song.
I would not feel my strength de - part, And then Thy ser - vice prove.
And la - bor up the heav'n - ly hill With wear - y feet and slow.
O not for Thee my fad - ing fires, The ash - es of my heart.
For Thee the glo - ry of my prime, The full - ness of my heart. A - men.

There is no distinction between Jew and Greek; the same Lord is
Lord of all/Rom 10:12

Olive Wise Spannaus

Slovak melody
arr Richard Hillert

1. Lord of all na - tions, grant me grace To love all
2. Break down the wall that would di - vide Your chil - dren,
3. Give me your cour - age, Lord, to speak When - ev - er
4. With your own love may I be filled And by your

men of ev - ery race, And in each fel - low - man to
Lord, on ev - ery side. Let me seek first my neigh - bor's
strong op - press the weak. Should I my - self the vic - tim
Ho - ly Spir - it willed, That all I touch what - e'er I

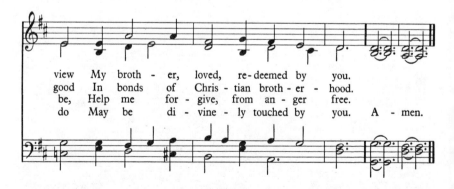

view My broth - er, loved, re - deemed by you.
good In bonds of Chris - tian broth - er - hood.
be, Help me for - give, from an - ger free.
do May be di - vine - ly touched by you. A - men.

This is my commandment, that you love one another as I have loved you/Jn 15:12

John 15:12   *Source unknown*

F
This is my commandment, that ye love one another,
   C7   F
  that your joy may be full. *(Repeat)*
  Bb   F
That your joy may be full,
   Bb   F
  That your joy may be full.

This is my commandment, that ye love one another,
   C   F
  that your joy may be full.

93 O Jesus Christ, Grow Thou in Me Commitment & Service

He must increase, but I must decrease/Jn 3:30

Johann C Lavater   *"Henry Greatorex Collection" (1851)*
tr Elizabeth L Smith   *Manoah*

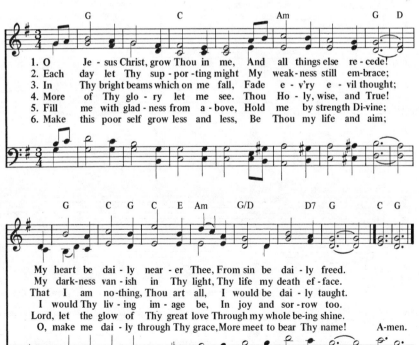

1. O Je-sus Christ, grow Thou in me, And all things else re-cede!
2. Each day let Thy sup-por-ting might My weak-ness still em-brace;
3. In Thy bright beams which on me fall, Fade e-v'ry e-vil thought;
4. More of Thy glo-ry let me see. Thou Ho-ly, wise, and True!
5. Fill me with glad-ness from a-bove, Hold me by strength Di-vine;
6. Make this poor self grow less and less, Be Thou my life and aim;

My heart be dai-ly near-er Thee, From sin be dai-ly freed.
My dark-ness van-ish in Thy light, Thy life my death ef-face.
That I am no-thing, Thou art all, I would be dai-ly taught.
I would Thy liv-ing im-age be, In joy and sor-row too.
Lord, let the glow of Thy great love Through my whole be-ing shine.
O, make me dai-ly through Thy grace, More meet to bear Thy name! A-men.

Jesus said to him, "I am the way, and the truth, and the life."/Jn 14:6

Tokuo Yamaguchi
para Everett M Stowe

Japanese gagaku mode
Isao Koizumi
Tokyo

1. Here, O Lord, your serv-ants gath-er, Hand we link with hand;
2. Man-y are the tongues we speak, Scat-tered are the lands,
3. Na-ture's se-crets o-pen wide, Chang-es nev-er cease;
4. Grant, O God, an age re-newed, Filled with death-less love,

Look-ing toward our Sav-ior's cross, Joined in love we stand.
Yet our hearts are one in God And his love's de-mands.
Where, O where, can wea-ry men Find the source of peace?
Help us as we work and pray, Send us from a-bove

As we seek the realm of God, We u-nite to pray:
E'en in dark-ness hope ap-pears, Call-ing age and youth:
Un-to all those sore dis-tressed, Torn by end-less strife:
Truth and cour-age, faith and power Need-ed in our strife:

Je-sus, Sav-ior, guide our steps, For you are the Way.
Je-sus, teach-er, dwell with us, For you are the Truth.
Je-sus, heal-er, bring your balm, For you are the Life.
Je-sus, Mas-ter, be our way, Be our truth, our life.

You have been set free from sin and have become slaves of God/Rom 6:22

George Matheson   *George William Martin*
Leominster

1. Make me a cap - tive, Lord, And then I shall be free; Force
2. My heart is weak and poor Un - til it mas - ter find; It
3. My pow'r is faint and low Till I have learned to serve; It
4. My will is not my own Till Thou hast made it Thine; If

me to ren - der up my sword, And I shall con - queror be. I
has no spring of ac - tion sure It var - ies with the wind; It
wants the need - ed fire to glow, It wants the breeze to nerve; It
it would reach a mon - arch's throne It must its crown re - sign; It

sink in life's a - larms When by my - self I stand, Im -
can - not free - ly move Till Thou hast wrought its chain; En -
can - not drive the world Un - til it - self be driven; Its
on - ly stands un - bent A - mid the clash - ing strife, When

pri - son me with - in Thine arms, And strong shall be my hand.
slave it with Thy match-less love, And death -less it shall reign.
flag can on - ly be un-furled When Thou shalt breathe from heav'n.
on Thy bos - om it has leant And found in Thee its life. A - men.

The LORD went before them by day in a pillar of cloud . . . and by night in a pillar of fire/Ex 13:21

William Williams
tr Peter Williams Gothers

John Hugh
Cwm Rhondda

1. Guide me, O thou great Je - ho - vah, Pil - grim through this
2. O - pen now the crys - tal foun - tain, Whence the heal - ing
3. When I tread the verge of Jor - dan, Bid my an - xious

bar - ren land; I am weak, but thou art might - y — Hold me
stream doth flow; Let the fire and cloud - y pil - lar Lead me
fears sub - side; Bear me through the swel - ling cur - rent, Land me

with thy pow'r - ful hand: Bread of hea - ven, Bread of hea - ven,
all my jour - ney through: Strong De - liv - 'rer, strong De - liv - 'rer,
safe on Ca - naan's side: Songs of prais - es, songs of prais - es

Feed me till I want no more, Feed me till I want no more.
Be thou still my strength and shield, Be thou still my strength and shield.
I will e - ver give to thee, I will e - ver give to thee. A - men.

For to me to live is Christ/Phil 1:21

Howard J Baer *Howard J Baer*

For Him I'll tell my broth - er. For

Him I'll spread the word. For Him I'll

give my life to serve Him day by

day. To Him I'll pray for oth - ers.

continued on next page

Declare his glory among the nations/Ps 96:3

Margaret Clarkson

Donald P Hustad
Janus

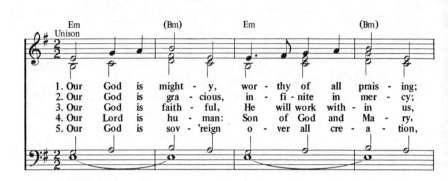

1. Our God is might - y, wor - thy of all prais - ing;
2. Our God is gra - cious, in - fi - nite in mer - cy;
3. Our God is faith - ful, He will work with - in us,
4. Our Lord is hu - man: Son of God and Ma - ry,
5. Our God is sov - 'reign o - ver all cre - a - tion,

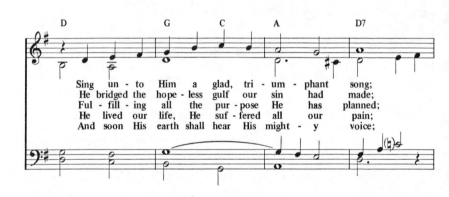

Sing un - to Him a glad, tri - um - phant song;
He bridged the hope - less gulf our sin had made;
Ful - fill - ing all the pur - pose He has planned;
He lived our life, He suf - fered all our pain;
And soon His earth shall hear His might - y voice;

He is the Lord, su - preme in earth and heav - en;
He gave His Son to pur - chase our sal - va - tion—
Cleans - ing our hearts and fill - ing with His Spir - it,
He bids us go to min - is - ter His mer - cy,
With shout of joy the King shall come in splen - dor—

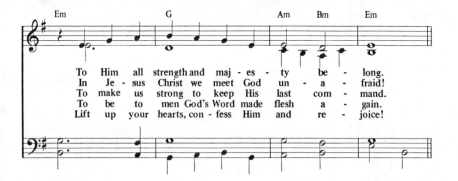

To Him all strength and maj - es - ty be - long.
In Je - sus Christ we meet God un - a - fraid!
To make us strong to keep His last com - mand.
To be to men God's Word made flesh a - gain.
Lift up your hearts, con - fess Him and re - joice!

Refrain

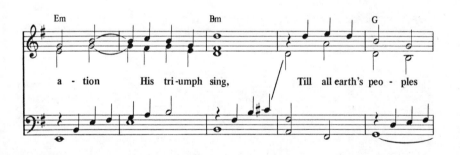

De - clare His glo - ry a - mong the na - tions; Through all cre -

a - tion His tri - umph sing, Till all earth's peo - ples

bow in ad-o - ra - tion, And Je - sus Christ be ev - er - last - ing King.

As thou didst send me into the world, so I have sent them into the world/Jn 17:18

William J Danker   *Ralph Vaughan Williams*
Sine Nomine

1. The send-ing, Lord, springs from Thy yearn-ing heart.   God, Thou the Send-er,
2. Thy bod-y paid   for those of ev - 'ry race;   To them we wit-ness,

5. One Mis-sion takes   me   o - ver land and sea   And   to the Chris-tian
6. From ur-ban deeps,   to   or - bits high in space, Through cross to glo - ry

Thou the Sent One art,   And of Thy mis - sion mak-est   us   a   part.
Christ, Thy bound-less grace,   With them one Bod - y, kneel be - fore Thy face.

broth - er next to   me.   Help me to   lis - ten, Lord, and speak for Thee.
moves one pil - grim race,   Prais - ing the Fa - ther, Son, and Spir - it's grace;

Al - le - lu - ia!   Al - le - lu - ia!

3. Where men their broth - ers heart - less - ly   op - press, Where peo - ple suf - fer,
4. One   man in need in bod - y, mind and soul; One word in   Je - sus'

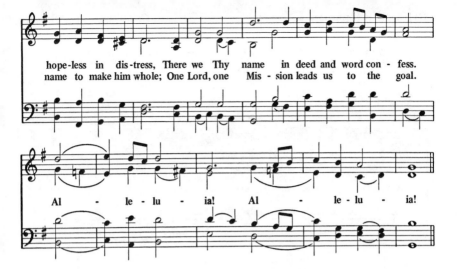

hope-less in dis-tress, There we Thy name in deed and word con - fess.
name to make him whole; One Lord, one Mis - sion leads us to the goal.

Al - le - lu - ia! Al - le - lu - ia!

100 For All the Saints

Commitment & Service

Therefore, since we are surrounded by so great a cloud
of witnesses... /Heb 12:1

William Walsham How

Ralph Vaughan Williams
Sine Nomine (hymn 99)

1. For all the saints who from their
labors rest,
Who Thee by faith before the world
confessed,
Thy name, O Jesus, be forever blest.
Alleluia! Alleluia!

2. Thou wast their rock, their fortress,
and their might,
Thou, Lord, their captain in the
well-fought fight;
Thou, in the darkness drear, their
one true light.
Alleluia! Alleluia!

3. O may Thy soldiers, faithful,
true and bold,
Fight as the saints who nobly
fought of old,
And win with them the victor's
crown of gold.
Alleluia! Alleluia!

4. O blest communion, fellowship divine!
We feebly struggle, they in glory shine;
Yet all are one in Thee, for all are Thine.
Alleluia! Alleluia!

5. And when the strife is fierce,
the warfare long,
Steals on the ear the distant triumph song,
And hearts are brave again, and arms
are strong.
Alleluia! Alleluia!

6. The golden evening brightens
in the west;
Soon, soon to faithful warriors
comes their rest;
Sweet is the calm of Paradise the blest.
Alleluia! Alleluia!

We rely on thee, and in thy name we have come/2 Chron 14:11

Edith G Cherry

Jean Sibelius
Finlandia

1. "We rest on Thee"–our Shield and our De - fen - der! We go not
2. Yea, "in Thy Name," O Cap - tain of sal - va - tion! In Thy dear
3. "We go" in faith, our own great weak-ness feel - ing, And need - ing
4. "We rest on Thee"–our Shield and our De - fen - der! Thine is the

forth a - lone a - gainst the foe; Strong in Thy strength, safe
Name, all oth - er names a - bove; Je - sus our Right - eous
more each day Thy grace to know: Yet from our hearts a
bat - tle, Thine shall be the praise When pas - sing through the

in Thy keep - ing ten - der, "We rest on Thee, and
ness, our sure foun - da - tion, Our Prince of glo - ry
song of tri - umph peal - ing; "We rest on Thee, and
gates of pear - ly splen - dor, Vic - tors— we rest with

in Thy Name we go," Strong in Thy strength, safe in Thy keep - ing
and our King of love, Je - sus our Right - eous - ness our sure foun
in Thy Name we go," Yet from our hearts a song of tri - umph
Thee, through end-less days, When pas - sing through the gates of pear - ly

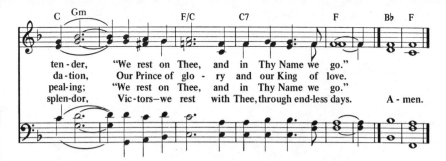

ten - der, "We rest on Thee, and in Thy Name we go."
da - tion, Our Prince of glo - ry and our King of love.
peal - ing; "We rest on Thee, and in Thy Name we go."
splen - dor, Vic - tors—we rest with Thee, through end - less days. A - men.

melody: "Finlandia" by Jean Sibelius. Used by permission of Breitkopf & Härtel, Wiesbaden; arrangement: from The Hymnal, copyright 1933, by the Presbyterian Board of Christian Education. Used by permission of The Westminster Press.

102 May the Mind of Christ My Savior Commitment & Service

Have this mind among yourselves, which is yours in Christ Jesus/Phil 2:5

Kate B Wilkinson

A Cyril Barham-Gould
St Leonards

1. May the mind of Christ my Sa - vior Live in me from day to day,
2. May the Word of God dwell rich - ly In my heart from hour to hour,
3. May the peace of God my Fa - ther Rule my life in e - v'ry thing,
4. May the love of Je - sus fill me, As the wa - ters fill the sea;
5. May I run the race be - fore me, Strong and brave to face the foe,
6. May His beau - ty rest up - on me As I seek the lost to win,

By His love and pow'r con - trol - ling All I do and say.
So that all may see I tri - umph On - ly thro' His pow'r.
That I may be calm to com - fort Sick and sor - row - ing.
Him ex - alt - ing, self a - bas - ing, This is vic - to - ry.
Look - ing on - ly un - to Je - sus As I on - ward go.
And may they for - get the chan - nel, See - ing on - ly Him. A - men.

words and music: by permission of the executors of Rev. C. Barham-Gould.

Cross Index to Hymns in *Hymns II*

A different tune to the same set of words is found in Hymns II.
#Words only are found in Urbana Praise.*

First Line Index

(Entries in italics are common titles)